ENGAGING STUDENTS THROUGH INQUIRY-ORIENTED LEARNING AND TECHNOLOGY

Teresa Coffman

Rowman & Littlefield Education
Lanham • New York • Toronto • Plymouth, UK

Published in the United States of America
by Rowman & Littlefield Education
A Division of Rowman & Littlefield Publishers, Inc.
A wholly owned subsidiary of
The Rowman & Littlefield Publishing Group, Inc.
4501 Forbes Boulevard, Suite 200, Lanham, Maryland 20706
www.rowmaneducation.com

Estover Road
Plymouth PL6 7PY
United Kingdom

Copyright © 2009 by Teresa Coffman

British Library Cataloguing in Publication Information Available

Library of Congress Cataloging-in-Publication Data

Coffman, Teresa, 1966–
  Engaging students through inquiry-oriented learning and technology /
Teresa Coffman.
    p. cm.
  ISBN 978-1-60709-069-4 (cloth : alk. paper) — ISBN 978-1-60709-070-0
(pbk. : alk. paper) — ISBN 978-1-60709-071-7 (electronic)
  1. Inquiry-based learning. 2. Web-based instruction. I. Title.
  LB1027.23.C635 2009
  371.39—dc22   2009018075

∞^{TM} The paper used in this publication meets the minimum requirements of
American National Standard for Information Sciences—Permanence of Paper
for Printed Library Materials, ANSI/NISO Z39.48-1992.
Manufactured in the United States of America.

CONTENTS

FOREWORD

The topic of inquiry learning and technology integration is one of great importance in our educational environment at this moment in time—important because we as educators are always seeking ways to effectively integrate technology into schools and classrooms in order to engage students in the process of learning and to better prepare them to be successful in this twenty-first-century environment.

Just by glancing at the table of contents for *Engaging Students through Inquiry-Oriented Learning and Technology*, a reader can see what inquiry learning looks like in a classroom enhanced by technology. In the chapters themselves, Coffman explains inquiry-based approaches to learning and helps the reader discover how to identify good inquiry-oriented questions to get students thinking about course content. Readers also embark on adventures in building good WebQuests, Web inquiry activities, and telecollaborative activities that engage students in the process of learning. Coffman leads the reader to explore ways to evaluate students and their inquiry-oriented activities, using technology tools such as the Internet, mind maps, and spreadsheets to analyze data and draw conclusions about meaningful relationships and connections between the learning objectives and the data. The blending of Web-based and computer-based applications makes these activities easy to integrate into most disciplines.

Educators are always asking for ways to make their instruction better. The answer is simply to ask more questions and to teach so that students ask more questions. As they draw on Coffman's expertise and insights in this text, educators will find ways to lead their students to deeper and higher levels of learning. This book is important to preservice teachers, practicing teachers, and administrators looking for professional development material for their teachers. It clearly communicates technology tools and inquiry-oriented learning approaches to the reader/educator, providing sound ideas and instructional strategies for easy integration into the classroom.

Juliette C. Mersiowsky

1

WHAT IS INQUIRY?

Welcome to the world of inquiry learning. Defined by experience and exploration, it involves students in the process of learning so they acquire a deeper understanding of the material being taught. Inquiry learning implements a constructivist approach so that students interact with the content by asking questions to increase understanding and comprehension and at the same time construct their own knowledge.

The inquiry approach to learning originates in science education, where students create and test a hypothesis (or problem) and throughout the process are encouraged to become actively involved in the discovery of information by highlighting both the usefulness and the application of the information itself. Throughout this process, students discover facts and develop a higher-order understanding of topics and ideas.

Inquiry is important to ensure that students are not only memorizing required factual information but are also applying the facts to the development of meaningful questions and to their own understanding. The questioning approach that is utilized throughout the inquiry process allows students to progress from simply holding and finding factual information to being able to apply new knowledge in novel and different ways.

As a teacher, you can develop inquiry skills in your students by help-ing them to develop a curiosity of the world around them and then to question and seek answers to help solve relevant problems. This is a real-world application of functional skills required to succeed in the world today—and very much needed by our twenty-first-century stu-dents.

OVERVIEW

In the classroom, inquiry-oriented learning can take many forms. Mov-ing away from traditional recitation, the inquiry approach to learning en-courages and helps students form their own questions and work through the process of answering them. For example, after a class studies the American Civil War, the teacher asks students to explore topics that are of unique interest to them. If a student has a special interest in horses, that student is then encouraged to further explore how horses played an important role in the Civil War. For example, the student might especially want to look at how generals Robert E. Lee and Stonewall Jackson chose their horses for battle in order to lead their soldiers and missions. The student learns at a deeper level, in this specific example, about the personalities and characteristics of the two generals and about the horses they owned. In so doing, the student learns key information about the Civil War that is of unique interest to him or her.

Through inquiry learning, students become actively involved in the in-quiry activity by incorporating information literacy skills into solving the problem. Skills such as observing, collecting, analyzing, and synthesizing information are developed in order to make predictions and draw con-clusions. Inquiry-oriented learning allows students to discover and pur-sue information with active and engaged involvement in the material.

As the teacher, you can help scaffold and build upon the inquiry process by assisting and encouraging students to ask questions related to the topic being investigated. Students then have the responsibility to identify and define their own individual procedures for answering these questions to make the content personal and meaningful to them.

In the Civil War example above, the student no longer sees the two generals as distant, historical figures. Through inquiry learning, the Civil

War and the two generals become real and significant. The student can now dig deeper into the content, ask meaningful questions, and explore the Civil War from a perspective of interest.

MOTIVATION AND INQUIRY

In student learning, motivation is a key element, and this is especially critical with inquiry activities. Without student motivation, engagement will not happen and deep inquiry will not take place. When motivated, students are eager to learn, fascinated by their discoveries, and enjoy asking questions.

Motivation is generally either intrinsic or extrinsic. *Intrinsic* motivation is internal and comes because we are interested in the material and want to do a good job. *Extrinsic* motivation, on the other hand, comes from external factors, such as good grades or praise on an assignment.

When you begin creating your inquiry activity, try to engage both forms of motivation equally. As shown in table 1.1, so that each inquiry activity builds on providing both intrinsic and extrinsic motivation, you want to ensure that the activity is meaningful, authentic, and challenging and at the same time aligns with your learning standards.

In order to create activities that aid in motivating your students, you want to make sure that the activity is meaningful and worthwhile. In developing class activities, it is important to ask yourself the following: Why is this important for my students to understand? How does this topic relate to their interests? How does this topic tie into their future?

Table 1.1. Motivation and Inquiry

Motivation	Examples
Intrinsic	• Authentic activities that are personal, meaningful, and challenging, and that question students' existing understanding. • Well-designed activities that encourage curiosity and provide students with some control over their own learning. • Students explore a "big idea" question about the content that is interesting to them (e.g., How did the generals of the Civil War choose the horses they did?).
Extrinsic	• Good grades and praise for quality work from teachers and classmates. • Thoughtful and reflective comments from the teacher and classmates to aid students and encourage investigation and exploration.

One way to highlight the importance of an activity and motivate your students is to provide connections to their current interests and concerns. For example, in a history class, have your students investigate how elections impact their lives. Voting can and does make a difference. It is critical to create an activity that connects your students to the content being explored and engages them in the discipline.

BLOOM'S TAXONOMY AND INQUIRY

Benjamin Bloom's taxonomy, updated in 2001, can help you identify and categorize good questions to guide student learning. Within the taxonomy, there are six cognitive levels, and these move from lower- to higher-order thinking. The six levels are remembering (knowledge), understanding (comprehension), applying, analyzing, evaluating, and creating (synthesizing).

These six levels provide opportunities for teachers to incorporate inquiry learning into their lessons beyond the lower cognitive-level thinking activities, such as knowledge and comprehension, that are centered on recitation and memorization.

In order to develop critical thinking and good inquiry activities, you want to ask questions that provide students with opportunities to apply, analyze, synthesize, and evaluate important concepts and themes within the activity. This deeper investigation and exploration of topics allows your students to focus on differentiating and questioning different points of view and then synthesize the information in order to debate an issue or build a model.

At any level within Bloom's taxonomy, your objective is to identify questions that engage your students and encourage them to ask more in-depth questions about the learning objectives. With Bloom's taxonomy, it is important that students remember key concepts and understand them, but more importantly you want them to also begin applying, analyzing, and evaluating complex ideas.

As you begin to think about creating learning activities within your lesson, you want to identify verbs to help guide you in the design of your questions and activities. See table 1.2 for an illustration of action verbs that could be used in applying Bloom's taxonomy to the Civil War example.

Table 1.2. Verbs and Inquiry

Taxonomy	Action Verbs	Question	Activity
Application	Construct	Can you apply the method used to some experience of your own?	Working with a classmate, *construct* a statistical model on the reliability of war strategies used by the generals.
Analysis	Investigate	What questions would you ask the generals of the American Civil War, knowing what you know now?	Working in small groups, write a letter to the Civil War generals to *investigate* their rationale for going into war.
Synthesis	Propose	What strategy could President Abraham Lincoln have proposed if he had been able to see into the future for America before the Civil War?	Working with a partner, draft a *proposal* that Abraham Lincoln could have submitted to Congress one month before the Civil War officially started.
Evaluation	Choose	What information is needed in order to defend your position for fighting in the American Civil War?	Working in small groups, create a Web site outlining key strategic moves *chosen* during the Civil War and how these strategies impacted the duration of the war and its effect on the American people.

By carefully choosing action verbs when designing your activities, you will incorporate good questions and guide your students' learning toward higher levels of thought about important topics being explored in your class.

INQUIRY LEARNING

As the teacher, you already use different types of inquiry learning. Historically, teacher-centered learning has been the most popular. Inquiry learning focuses on you asking questions on a consistent basis to ensure that your students understand the material during a class discussion.

Now, let's step this process up a bit by getting your students actively involved. You will ask questions and your students will also ask questions by working with their classmates to explore and discover possible answers.

A second type of inquiry learning is student centered. Within this structure of learning, students bring their unique knowledge, understanding, and skills to the learning community. The focus is on the student, with an emphasis placed on active engagement in the learning process to develop and build on student understanding. Through questioning and discovering information, the student learns the material. The teacher sets up the activity and facilitates the process to ensure students are on task and learning what is intended.

Inquiry follows a process similar to that shown in figure 1.1. The process begins with questioning and moves through discovery, exploration, and presentation of findings. Throughout this dynamic process,

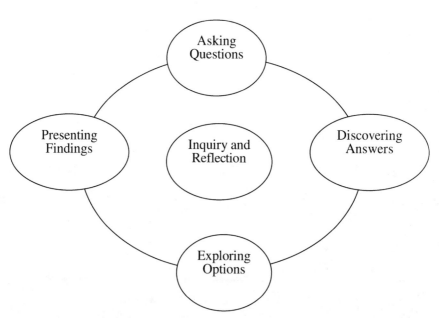

Figure 1.1.   Inquiry Process

questions are introduced, hypotheses are tested, and new questions are formed and reformed. Central to this inquiry process is reflection and feedback from the teacher and classmates to ensure that understanding and learning are occurring.

This is a cyclical process that is in continuous movement between each phase. For this reason, it is necessary to have a project structure in place before inquiry-oriented activities begin. Good planning begins with a clearly identified "big idea" that aligns with the instructional standard.

INQUIRY-ORIENTED LEARNING ACTIVITIES

Inquiry-oriented learning involves any activity that encourages students to think, ask questions, explore information, and then present possible solutions or ideas. This book explores WebQuests, Web inquiry, and telecollaborative activities as inquiry-oriented learning activities that can be implemented in the classroom to engage students in their learning process. Each activity is similar because each uses the Internet to discover and explore as well as share information.

With the WebQuests, Web inquiry, and telecollaborative activities incorporated into your classroom, your students will have a variety of opportunities to construct their own understanding of topics as they are explored in class. Through the process of inquiry, your students will be engaged, motivated, and eager to learn new ideas and concepts.

The inquiry process involves:

- Identifying questions to ask to find possible answers.
- Identifying appropriate and quality resources to aid students in answering the identified questions.
- Manipulating resources to ensure that correct information is identified and answers to specific questions are explored.
- Formulating answers discovered and identifying how these answers relate back to the original questions.

Your role as the teacher in the inquiry process is to create meaningful activities that engage your students and capture their attention so they are motivated to learn and discover information by asking questions and then sharing that new knowledge with others in meaningful ways.

WebQuests

A WebQuest is an inquiry-oriented activity that primarily uses the Internet for resources. WebQuests are generally developed around a theme. For example, you can have students create a newspaper that highlights the times of Christopher Columbus and the story of Columbus, particularly his quest for India. The newspaper can also compare and contrast Columbus's experiences to those of other explorers past and present.

WebQuests can be completed individually or in small groups. If done in a group setting, students can role play different characters or be assigned different topics within the overall theme, such as the example of the newspaper. Students are assigned roles such as the Queen, Columbus, ship reporters, and people in the Americas, and they then gather and report on their specific role during that time period.

This diverse learning experience described above provides students with opportunities to learn about and tell the individual stories of each role and then share their findings in the format of a newspaper that can be published either on the Internet or in the school newspaper to share with others.

In a WebQuest, students are provided with questions and resources that they use in order to discover and explore information. Students then present their findings. See the "Out at Sea WebQuest" feature for a detailed example of a quest and inquiry.

OUT AT SEA WEBQUEST

You are in charge of the ship's "Journey Journal." The journal contains many different items. You need to complete all the tasks and put the information together in a Journey Journal notebook.

Step 1: Biographical Information on the Explorer

In order to do a good job for your Captain, you must understand who he or she is. Let's start by first watching a short video about explorers in general. *Watch the video.*

Now that you know more about explorers of the world, it is time to concentrate on your explorer. Click on the *Explorer Worksheet* and answer all the questions about your assigned explorer. Next, you will share your findings about your explorer with the class so make sure you print out your report and place it in your "Journey Journal."

Step 2: Cargo and Food Report

As you set sail for the exploration, you must make sure that your ship's cargo list is complete.

Ensure that the ship is fully stocked with food for your crew for the long voyage. Gather information about foods that were available during the time period of your explorer and design a list of items you will need for your ship. Make sure you address such questions as:

What will the crew drink?
Will you stop along the way to get more food?
Will you fish or hunt for food?

What else will you bring on your voyage? Investigate what else your explorer might have brought with him or her by thinking about what kind of clothes were needed, types of tools needed, trading trinkets, or any other items you discover.

When you have your ship's Cargo and Food Report, add it to your "Journey Journal."

Step 3: Navigator Report

Now that your ship is fully stocked, it is time to set sail. But how will the Captain know where to go? Well, as his or her first mate, it is your job to make sure the Captain has the appropriate maps and directions to reach the destination.

First, determine how explorers navigated their ships during this time period and report your findings so that the Captain can have those instruments on the ship when it sets sail.

Second, create a map of the journey the explorer took to reach his or her destination. Print out a world map that shows where your explorer began and the route taken to reach the final destination. Make sure you label your map with the following information (a map Web site is available for your use):

- Country that the ship started its voyage in.
- Country where the ship ended its voyage.
- The body of water the ship traveled across.
- The Equator and the different hemispheres.
- Draw a navigational symbol showing North, South, East, and West.

Also, draw a picture of the ship and what it must have looked like when it landed at its destination. Don't forget to take note of such things as wildlife or rivers in your drawing.

Add all these items to your "Journey Journal."

Step 4: Achievements of Explorer Report

LAND Aheeeeeaaaad . . .
You have safely made it to your destination!
Now as the first mate, it is your responsibility to act as the reporter to report back to the homeland new discoveries such as:

- Where did you land?
- What did you find?
- Were there any native people there?
- Who are they and what are they like?
- Are there raw materials to build homes or survive? What kind of homes might you build?
- Are there plants to eat or should seed be sent over on future voyages?
- What kind of wildlife is there?
- Is this the final destination of the explorer, or does he or she set sail soon afterward and explore further?

> The King and Queen are very curious people, so your report must be detailed. Your report should be about two pages in length. It should tell of your adventure and the discovery of this new land and what it has to offer. Don't forget to include in your report at least two drawings of your findings so they can see what this new land looks like.
>
> Add all these items to your "Journey Journal."

WebQuests can be completed in varying lengths of time, from one or two class periods to an entire unit of instruction. Activities include collecting and then sharing information. The information can be disseminated and shared through preparation for a debate or presentation, writing an editorial to be published in the local paper, or presenting at the next parent conference or community meeting. As its name implies, this is a *Quest*. Therefore, it should be fun, informative, exciting, and engaging as well as inquiry based.

Web Inquiry

Web inquiry activities are not as involved or in-depth as WebQuests. Web inquiry activities look at raw data. From these data, students explore and make predictions based on their analysis. The teacher is responsible for identifying the questions, and the students are responsible for identifying the specific procedures and strategies for obtaining the appropriate information for the questions posed.

Web inquiry is a form of guided inquiry and therefore it is important to provide appropriate resources to help students answer content questions. At the same time, students should also be encouraged to find additional resources to help answer the questions posed.

Through Web inquiry, students learn how to manipulate and explore raw data with the resources provided by the teacher. They are then guided toward finding the information requested through structured scaffolding.

For example, a student studying economics could be directed by the teacher to the Department of Labor's Bureau of Labor Statistics Web site at www.bls.gov/ to find actual data on labor in the local area and statistics related to the economy. These are the actual data that economists look at to make decisions and create meaning around many important decisions regarding the U.S. economy.

Telecollaborative Activities

Telecollaborative activities are another form of inquiry-oriented learning that additionally involves students collecting and sharing data. The main difference with this activity as opposed to WebQuests or Web inquiry projects is that during a telecollaborative activity, students collect and share data with other students, outside experts, and other teachers in different locations (outside the classroom) using Internet collaboration and communication tools.

Students have the ability to work collaboratively with you and other students as well as with experts around the world to solve workable and at times complex problems. This inquiry-oriented activity links your students and resources together so they can identify key questions from data collected around the world. The key idea is working collaboratively using the Internet with individuals outside of the classroom.

For example, students in a science class could participate in a global experiment to determine how much water they use every day and then compare that to how much water communities around the world use each day at CIESE, the Center for Innovation in Engineering and Science Education, at www.ciese.org/collabprojs.html. Questions are posed such as: "Do you think people in other parts of the world use more or less water than you?" This exercise gets students engaged and excited about learning.

In the chapters that follow, WebQuests, Web inquiry, and telecollaborative activities will be explored in depth, enabling you to develop and utilize these inquiry tools in your classroom to support and enhance inquiry-oriented learning. Inquiry-oriented learning is an important and effective way to teach and learn. Not only will you enjoy this student-centered approach, but your students will too.

Inquiry-oriented learning is also an exciting way for you as the teacher to share with your students knowledge that exists outside the classroom. It also provides opportunities for encouraging students to develop the twenty-first-century skills they need in today's world.

Using an inquiry-oriented learning approach allows your students to:

- Explore and discover content through an authentic and challenging learning context.
- Create and test a hypothesis through authentic and real-world tools.
- Learn and explore content within a collaborative environment.
- Gain self-efficacy with prior knowledge and expand new knowledge.
- Use technology to enhance and strengthen higher-order thinking.

PROMOTING AND APPLYING INQUIRY IN YOUR CLASSROOM

To promote inquiry in the classroom, you want to first identify "big ideas" in the content being explored. Big ideas are overarching questions that guide the instruction, emphasize the main idea of the unit, and are connected to the learning standards. Once big ideas are identified, encourage students to identify subquestions, plan and conduct investigations, and work in small groups to identify solutions or possible answers to the questions posed.

For example, in a unit that teaches sixth graders about economics, specifically a learning standard that looks at the relationship between money and different societies throughout the world, a big idea question could be: "How have money and other means of commerce taken shape throughout history and across different civilizations?"

In the classroom, the teacher would lead a brainstorming session by posing this question and guiding students to think about how money and bartering have changed throughout societies. As students are brainstorming, the teacher's role is to write all of the students' ideas on an interactive board.

Once students finish suggesting ideas, select students can come up to the interactive board to organize the collection of ideas into categories. Once the categories are organized, you can have students brainstorm possible subquestions for each category. Once subquestions are identified, as a collective group the class can then decide which questions and categories they want to work on and understand better.

In small groups or as a class, students can then begin their inquiry. The notes of this brainstorming session can be saved and posted to the

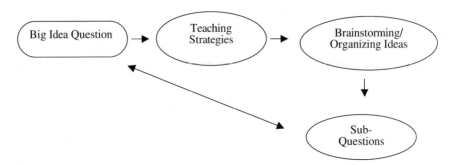

Figure I.2. Questioning Process

class Web site so everyone has a reference point to stay connected to the overall goal of the activity. Figure 1.2 outlines the questioning process.

As this example illustrates, throughout the inquiry process you want your students to be involved in their own learning. This is true for all inquiry projects. Inquiry learning allows students to develop strategies and methods for deep investigation and exploration into important topics explored in class as they relate to the students' world. Through this process, you are teaching your students how to ask questions and how to be involved in their learning process. Inquiry-oriented learning is not passive; rather, it is an active and engaged process that leads to higher-order thinking.

Throughout the inquiry process, students work in collective groups and as a class to identify what they already know about a given topic as well as what they do not know. As the teacher, it is your responsibility to encourage students to identify key points about the topic that are of interest to them personally and to begin asking deeper questions to explore their interests further as they relate to the intended learning objective. Through this process of collaboration and investigation, students begin to understand the big idea of the lesson and the larger picture— their personal world. Inquiry learning is beginning to take shape.

Taking Care of Your Students

Although inquiry activities are student centered, your students need guidance from you as they work. As the teacher, you want to ensure that students receive guidance in the activity as well as have plenty of opportunities for practice and feedback.

Traditionally, teaching has focused on dispensing knowledge and information to students through lecture, memorization, and skill-specific tasks. Once students complete a specific task, they complete a paper, a presentation, and/or an objective test.

In an inquiry assignment, the teacher provides students with an open-ended question, a big idea question. From there, students are encouraged to ask further questions and are provided good resources and tools. Students are often placed into small homogeneous groups so they can conduct research, ask questions, and ultimately present their findings in meaningful ways, such as a debate, an editorial for the school paper, or a letter to a community leader to share information on a political or social topic.

Through this inquiry-activity process, you eventually want your students to take the lead in asking questions, investigating good resources, and identifying solutions. However, to fully focus and engage them in the learning process, each activity must begin with a big idea question. This question must capture your students' attention and encourage them to ask follow-up questions, make predictions, and discover new information.

A big idea question such as "What happens if an animal or plant is removed from the food web?" allows students to creatively explore this science concept from a broad perspective and to think more critically about food webs in general. Ultimately, it allows students to see how this web impacts life in general. Additional layers to this question can be added to the original big idea question as students develop explanations, evaluate predictions, and further expand their understanding.

Now you try it. Use table 1.3 to formulate a big idea question and then relate it back to your course-content standards and learning objectives. Prepare two big idea questions that you want your students to investigate and explore, identify which content standards your questions align with, and then list objectives that are met with these two inquiry explorations.

In this approach, students are encouraged to:

- Become self-directed learners intrinsically motivated through their discoveries.

Table 1.3. Big Idea Questions

Big Idea Question	Content Standards	Learning Objectives
1.		
2.		

- Work collaboratively with classmates through cooperative learning strategies and methods.
- Become actively engaged in the learning activity and task at hand.
- Share new knowledge through a presentation or performance.
- Develop higher-order thinking skills.

Creativity and Inquiry

Inquiry-oriented learning is a creative form of learning in which students take an active role and are guided by you the teacher. You need to provide questions about course objectives as well as provide resources to ensure a rich learning environment where your students are actively engaged in critical thinking and creativity. Through inquiry, the focus is on the big picture of the learning unit: "Why is this important to me?"

Throughout this process, you should:

- Create an authentic and meaningful task. This task must be wrapped around the most important concepts from your activity or unit that you want your students to know.
- Implement continued and authentic assessments that include real-world tasks that demonstrate understanding and knowledge creation.
- Identify the educational goals of the lesson along with appropriate objectives.

- Facilitate inquiry throughout the learning process to guide students in higher-order thinking by having students question and reflect on their findings.
- Be comfortable learning along with your students.

TWENTY-FIRST-CENTURY SKILLS

As you develop and identify the big idea for your unit and learning objective, you should also think about how to integrate twenty-first-century skills into your learning unit. Planning for inquiry projects goes beyond having students achieve content knowledge; planning should also engage students into practicing higher-order thinking skills, such as applying, analyzing, synthesizing, and evaluating information in order to create a new understanding of knowledge.

Inquiry-oriented activities have the potential to provide students with opportunities to develop these necessary skills by encouraging them to work on problems and identify questions to determine possible solutions. The idea is for you to ask questions that your students are concerned about and then to tie these questions into course standards.

When educators talk about twenty-first-century skills and preparing students for the world outside of a school's traditional four walls, the emphasis is on developing creative thinkers and self-directed risk takers who are able to ask thoughtful questions. Inquiry-oriented learning creates an open and collaborative environment so that students can work in small and large groups inside and outside the classroom to develop skills that will enable them to be successful in the world around them.

Through carefully planned activities, students are taught how to prioritize investigations and discoveries by working closely with team members and the teacher. Students have opportunities to solve problems using tools that experts in the field use.

For example, if students are creating a food web habitat in a science course, small groups are formed to look for evidence of specific impact on ecosystems and habitats when a plant or an animal has changed in that habitat. Each small group works on a food web identifying their hypotheses as to what changes in the habitat if the web is altered.

Then groups look for evidence using online databases to collect real-world data to support their specific hypotheses. This type of active and engaged learning stimulates and excites students and ultimately promotes knowledge.

INFORMATION TECHNOLOGY AND INQUIRY LEARNING

Inquiry-learning lessons focus on the big idea as identified by the teacher. It is from this big idea that your students create a hypothesis. The central focus is for students to begin asking relevant questions and begin the process of research and discovery. Using the food web example, the teacher could show a video and have a discussion, or create a Wiki to work collaboratively and then share new knowledge with others outside the class.

Students could also keep a reflection journal of their new knowledge on a class blog that could be shared with other classes and parents to explain about elements of a food web and the importance of the interrelationships. Next, the whole class could talk about how scientists use analogies and comparisons to make predictions and then develop theories.

Technology provides an effective and engaging way for students to become investigators of knowledge and to help them create new understandings of course topics. The power of technology tools are that they allow students to communicate with their teachers, classmates, and other students as well as experts outside the classroom in a global context.

Technology tools, such as the Internet, and software programs, such as presentation software, allow student-collected data to be stored and shared and then presented in new and meaningful ways.

Technology tools allow opportunities for students to:

- Create mental images through concept maps and electronic journals.
- Explore databases with raw data and primary source documents, images, and films.
- Communicate with other students in the classroom or the school, as well as with students in other locations around the country or world.

- Ask experts in the area of study that the students are investigating to get a real-world perspective on an issue or concept.

Most importantly, technology tools provide opportunities for students to investigate and explore the world just as professionals do out in the field. And this real-world learning and application are exactly what the inquiry-oriented approach to learning is all about.

SUMMARY

In this chapter, key elements found in inquiry-oriented activities were identified. The primary goal in inquiry learning is to pose a question that relates to the standards of learning as well as student interests. Questions should be broad and at the same time answerable. Activities should provide students with opportunities to create hypotheses and then test their hypotheses in small homogeneous groups. Throughout an activity, students should have ample opportunity to reflect on their understandings and share this new knowledge with their classmates. By the end of an activity, students have a product that can be shared with others. In the next chapter, we will look at objectives and how teachers can align standards to inquiry-oriented questions.

FURTHER INVESTIGATION

Bloom, B. S. (1956). *Taxonomy of Educational Objectives, Handbook I: The Cognitive Domain*. New York: David McKay.

Bransford, J., Brown, A., & Cocking, R. Eds. (1999). *How People Learn*. National Research Council, Washington, D.C.: National Academy Press. www.nap.edu/openbook/0309065577/html/index.html.

Connect to the Classroom: Inquiry-Based Learning. www.thirteen.org/edonline/concept2class/inquiry/index.html.

Exploratorium: The Museum of Science, Art, and Human Perception at the Palace of Fine Arts. www.exploratorium.edu.

Integration: Building 21st-Century Learning Environments. www.landmarkproject.com/edtechnot_warlick/.

Krathwohl, D. R., Bloom, B. S., & Masia, B. B. (1973). *Taxonomy of Educational Objectives: The Classification of Educational Goals, Handbook II: The Affective Domain*. New York: David McKay.

Learning for the 21st Century. http://21stcenturyskills.org/downloads/P21_ Report.pdf.

YouthLearn: An Introduction to Inquiry-Based Learning. www.youthlearn. org/learning/approach/inquiry.asp.

REFLECTION

1. How can you integrate inquiry-oriented teaching and learning into the way you presently teach?
2. What does it mean to incorporate big idea questions into your classroom projects? List a big idea question for a unit you are planning to teach within the next month.
3. Identify teaching and learning strategies you can use to engage your students in exploring your big idea question.

2

SETTING UP AN ACTIVITY: TYING
GOOD QUESTIONS TO OBJECTIVES

In chapter 1, you were introduced to inquiry-oriented learning. The importance of "big idea" questions and the need for meaningful activities to ensure students are achieving understanding as well as creating meaning from each task were discussed. In chapter 2, we explore how to write objectives, specifically the need to identify meaningful learning objectives in order to design an inquiry-oriented lesson.

OVERVIEW

The premise of inquiry learning is that students assume a leading role in their own learning. This is similar to a constructivist's view of teaching and learning. In adopting this approach, teachers may get the impression that creating instructional objectives is unnecessary if students are to be in charge of their own learning. However, the very opposite is true. Teachers do need to identify goals and objectives.

When inquiry learning is integrated into your classroom, planning must be a priority in the process. Goals and objectives need to be identified, lesson plans developed, quality resources found, and "big idea" questions developed. When you set the stage with these preparatory steps, students have a better understanding of the learning process and the content, and are therefore more engaged and ready to embark on their learning experience.

PLANNING STAGE

Each part of an inquiry-oriented activity should serve a purpose and have clear goals. Planning is the first step in the inquiry process. Throughout your design process, you should always go back to your objectives to ensure that you are creating a learning activity that is on task with your stated goals. This helps to ensure the outcome and that the task your students are engaged in is authentic and relevant work.

When creating an inquiry-oriented activity, you want students to take the lead, but there must be a clear path with well-identified strategies to allow them to be successful and to explore topics beyond simply the fact-finding missions of past. One way to do this is to identify what you want your students to understand from this activity and what you want them to "take away" in terms of knowledge gained.

Objectives and assessments can then be identified to ensure that students remain on task and are able to articulate why the lesson is important and what goals are necessary for them to achieve. By identifying these critical take-aways, you begin to think about essential learning outcomes and how relationships can be developed and built on main concepts.

This is accomplished by looking at the standards of learning (SOLs) for your topic and deciphering what the big picture is and how best to identify the importance of this picture to your students.

For example, below are two SOLs. Identify the take-away from each.

Standards of Learning:

SOL1: Using appropriate technology, students will solve problems in mathematics.

SOL2: Students will represent and interpret the relationships between quantities algebraically.

Take-Away:

1. Technology can aid in solving these types of algebraic problems.
2. Variables, such as x and y, can be used to represent unknown quantities in algebraic expressions.

Next, learning objectives can be written that identify what students will understand and the resultant take-away from the lesson.

Students will:

- Use spreadsheet software to simulate algebraic expressions and post their reflections on the class blog to share with experts in the field of mathematics.

Students will:

- Compare and contrast numeric and algebraic expressions.
- Evaluate algebraic expressions, given that the value represented by variables (non-numeric letters) represents the unknown.

Write a real-world problem to represent the algebraic expression.

After identifying both the take-away and the objective for each SOL, it is now time to provide opportunities for students to dig deeper into the content. Instructional strategies can be created that allow students to think critically about the concepts by analyzing and exploring various algebraic expressions. The new knowledge and understanding of mathematical variables gained can then be presented in meaningful ways. See the "Sample Activity in a Mathematics Classroom" feature.

The main point of this exercise is to:

1. Identify SOLs.
2. Determine the take-away for each SOL.
3. Establish learning objectives for each.

SAMPLE ACTIVITY IN A MATHEMATICS CLASSROOM

In a large group discussion, introduce new concepts of mathematical variables and algebraic expressions.

Goal: Introduce the meaning of this new algebraic language to students and connect this language to their personal lives.

Activity: Have students in the class write down something they are wearing, such as jeans or tennis shoes. This will be their value of expression.

Then, as a group identify variables for each article identified. For example:

n = necklace
w = watch
s = shirt
j = jeans

Ask students to raise their hands if they wrote down jeans as their value of expression. Write the number next to j. Repeat with necklaces, watches, and shirts.

5j   6n   10w   8s

Through this activity, the importance of variables has been determined and students are now beginning to identify reasons and application for the mathematical expressions.

The expression, 5j, is not simply "5j"; rather, it represents in mathematical form five students in the class who identified jeans as the item of clothing they are wearing.

Here is an example on a lesson concerning the U.S. Constitution:

Responsibility of the teacher:
Identify why the study of the U.S. Constitution and three branches of government is important for students and what is central for them to understand.

Questions to consider:

- What are the most important concepts for students to understand from this unit?
- What is important for students to remember about this unit a year from now?
- What observable behaviors do I want students to demonstrate and which cognitive domains will be evident?

By identifying what is important about the lesson, the teacher is forced to break down the unit into meaningful learning tasks and ultimately essential questions. For example, in the above illustration, it is important that students know the three branches of government and how each branch of government is tied to the U.S. Constitution and to them as U.S. citizens.

Once the teacher identifies what is important for students to understand, then a big idea question can be identified and necessary objectives of the lesson established. Objectives are the road map for students to take. They stipulate how students will identify and explore the big idea question.

To begin identifying an objective, you must first identify a learning standard. It is at this stage that you should also begin to think about which technology tool can best be used to enhance student learning during the exploration and presentation of new knowledge. Table 2.1 provides an outline of the process for this example.

Objectives provide a road map for students to answer the big idea question. This road map is not limited but instead provides a structure to help students develop a good understanding of the big idea question and know what the expectations are for the lesson and what is important to understand at the completion of the lesson.

When teachers provide open-ended big idea questions, students are provided with opportunities to explore the topic in depth. It also has potential for students to dig deeper into the content and go beyond a general understanding of the topic. When teachers provide clear objectives and learning goals, they provide a clear path for students to take in their inquiry task.

The idea of an inquiry-oriented activity is to go beyond the knowledge domain outlined by Benjamin Bloom, the educational theorist discussed

Table 2.1. Identifying the Objective and Big Idea Question

Topic	U.S. Constitution and the Three Branches of Government
Standards	The student will demonstrate knowledge of the American constitutional government by: • Explaining the relationship of state governments to the national government in the federal system. • Describing the structure and powers of local, state, and national governments. • Explaining the principle of separation of powers and the operation of checks and balances by identifying the procedures for amending the Constitution of the United States. The student will use technology to locate, evaluate, and collect information from a variety of sources. The student will use technology resources for solving problems and making informed decisions.
Goal	Students will understand how the Constitution of the United States impacts citizens. They will do this through interviews, analyzing primary source documents, and using digital images, video, and sound files to tell a story about how the U.S. Constitution plays a role in their lives.
Objective	Using primary source documents, design a story about the three branches of the U.S. government and how each branch impacts your day-to-day life in the United States.
Big Idea Question	How are the U.S. Constitution and the three branches of government related to each other?
Technology Tools *Described in chapter 7	Example technology tools that could engage students in answering these questions: • A MindMap Tool to highlight and provide a visual of the major concepts identified between branches of government and the U.S. Constitution. • Online database housing primary sources (images, letters, the Constitution, sound files, video) to read the Constitution of the United States and to review images of places and artifacts. • Multimedia (video, Web authoring, hyperstudio, podcasting) to combine artifacts, findings, and analysis to present understandings. • A Web site to post a presentation for parents and other students in different locations to view and ask questions about.

in chapter 1. He outlined taxonomy of learning objectives and important steps to get students to move toward higher-order thinking skills, such as application, analysis, synthesis, and evaluation of content, as students work on classroom activities.

Objectives should identify these skills and highlight what the expectations are for each student. For example, an inquiry-oriented objective for the above activity in a third-grade class could be as follows:

> The student will create a coloring book identifying and explaining each branch of the government and how each branch checks and balances one another and the relationship of the three government branches to the U.S. Constitution. When complete, post this coloring book on the Web for other classes to learn from.

THE INQUIRY PROCESS: QUESTIONS TO CONSIDER

In developing a lesson about the U.S. Constitution, questions need to be carefully considered by you, the teacher, when designing the inquiry activity. This ensures that the inquiry process is achieved for each student and the class as a whole.

1. Identify and list the specific skills you want students to develop when working on an inquiry-oriented activity.
   - Do you want students to practice and develop research skills?
   - What steps do you want students to take when synthesizing information gathered?
   - What strategies will you use to provide students with the necessary skills on research and synthesis?
   - How will you make these specific skills and knowledge relate to the identified learning standards and lesson objectives?
   - How will students work as a collaborative group?
2. What built-in methods will you use to evaluate students' understanding throughout the lesson?
   - How will you and your students collect data and information to provide an overview of student learning?
   - What questions can you ask students throughout the activity to ensure they are on track and are learning what is important?
3. How will you provide a real-world experience that gives students the opportunity to explore the big idea question of the activity?

- In the Constitution example, primary source documents can be used to provide students with a real-world context by providing them with the same tools a historian would use to solve such a problem.
- What strategies would help students reinforce this new understanding? Determine how a historian would investigate this big idea question and then provide students with opportunities to build these same skills.
- Introduce the question by having students brainstorm about the laws and ideas of their community, state, and U.S. government.
- Encourage students to think about past lessons by having students complete a KWL (What I Know) Chart.
- What types of technology tools will enhance student understanding?

4. Identify quality resources that provide students with the necessary information to explore the big idea question and help them develop a good understanding of the overall goal of the lesson itself.
   - Are the resources appropriate for the identified learning standards and objectives?
   - Will the resources help students solve the big idea question effectively?

5. Identify any distractions or problems that students may encounter when they work on the inquiry-oriented activity. Whether the distracters are new terms, complex resources, or new ideas, you will want to work through possible strategies to overcome these distracters or potential problems to ensure that students succeed in their inquiry task. Determine the abilities of your students, such as their knowledge of the subject, the level of their research skills, and their overall understanding of the task.
   - Is this activity appropriate for my students?
   - Develop strategies to ensure that all students are successful in the activity.

Table 2.2 provides a template to note key questions and issues important for you to consider when designing your inquiry-oriented activity.

Table 2.2. Key Questions Template

Questions to consider based on your inquiry development activity	
Specific big ideas you want your students to achieve	For example, English teachers may want students to be fluent in language. Big Idea Question: How do authors use different elements of a story to create mood?
Methods of evaluation (informal and formal)	What would be sufficient for my students to perform to demonstrate their understanding? • Develop a brochure to help younger students understand what is meant by different elements of story used by authors to create mood. Ask questions and observe to ensure students are thinking about the big idea question and are on task.
Real-world experiences you will provide	How can I incorporate relevancy into my unit? Students can create a Wiki book highlighting understandings. Authors can comment and participate through the invitation of students.
Resources you have reviewed	What resources can I provide to engage students in the important concepts I want them to discover? • ReadWriteThink.org • Character Graphic Organizers Worksheet • Story Moods Graphic Organizer Worksheet • Young Authors Narrative Conference • Wikispaces.org
Distractions your students may encounter	What types of distractions will students encounter that might keep them from understanding the big idea questions posed? • Students may remember topics studied but not understand the importance of the different concepts of mood and storytelling. Make sure activities focus students on important concepts.

At the conclusion of the inquiry-oriented activity, your students should be able to identify what was significant about the big idea question and how this new knowledge can be applied to past and future lessons. At the end of the lesson, students should also identify any confusion or disagreements they have with the information and be able to articulate how this new knowledge relates to their personal experiences.

TECHNOLOGY TOOLS AND THE BIG IDEA INVESTIGATION

The main rationale for integrating technology into an inquiry-oriented activity is to provide opportunities for students to experience and explore topics in a real-world context. It also helps with application. Exploring a library database to find resources and search terms aids students in answering the big idea question. Critically evaluating resources found on the Internet to determine their credibility and reliability before using the information in a presentation helps students form critical-analysis skills.

Additionally, students can analyze raw data found on the Internet at government Web sites such as the U.S. Census Bureau or National Oceanic and Atmospheric Administration (NOAA) to place in a spreadsheet or word-processing program to answer outlined questions. Or experts can be contacted at the Census Bureau and NOAA to help clarify specific questions students encounter from their data manipulation. In each of these examples, technology is used as a tool to communicate, research, analyze, and ultimately present new information.

In the chapters that follow, further exploration into inquiry-oriented activities utilizing technology will be provided, specifically creating a WebQuest and Web inquiry and telecollaborative activities using the Internet and technology tools to engage students in the process of learning.

SUMMARY

In this chapter, we explored the importance of ensuring that your learning objectives and learning goals were the central theme of your inquiry activity. As the teacher, you must have a clear understanding of what is important for students to understand and then be able to create a good big idea question around that intended understanding. You also want to provide relevancy to the activity by tying in authentic connections to the learning goal and tasks.

Next, you want to make sure that you incorporate good teaching strategies as well as constructive feedback and reflection to ensure that students remain focused, engaged, and on task. Finally, you want to integrate technology tools into the activity to provide real-world relevancy and application for students. Technology can be utilized for communication, research, analysis, and presentation.

FURTHER INVESTIGATION

Big Ideas. http://www.authenticeducation.org/bigideas/.

Bloom, B. S. (1984). *Taxonomy of Educational Objectives*. Boston: Allyn & Bacon.

From Now On: The Question Is the Answer. http://fno.org/oct97/question. html.

From Now On: Promoting Thinking and the Growth of Thinkers. http:// fnopress.com/pedagogy/modules/toc.htm.

Goetz, E., Alexander, P., & Ash, M. (1992). Understanding and Enhancing Students' Cognitive Processes. In *Educational Psychology: A Classroom Perspective*. New York: Merrill.

REFLECTION

1. Determine a big idea question that you can use for your next lesson.
2. Identify standards of learning (SOLs) that align with your big idea question.
3. List objectives to provide students with a road map to this big idea question and highlight your standard.
4. Identify the cognitive domains students will acquire while working on this activity.
5. Identify possible misunderstandings students may have in this inquiry-oriented activity.
6. Determine teaching strategies to aid students in their overall understanding of the big idea question.

SKILL-BUILDING ACTIVITY

Throughout chapter 2, we explored inquiry and how inquiry is built on a big idea question. The central focus was on engaging your students in an interesting and doable question that they are motivated to critically think about and discover new information about. Your goal at the conclusion of this chapter is to create a big idea question that aligns with your learning standards and is developed around an interesting and doable problem that really grabs your students' interest.

CREATING A WEBQUEST

WebQuests have become very popular in education. What exactly are they? A WebQuest is an inquiry-oriented activity where most if not all of the resources that your students explore and analyze are provided on the Internet. The goal of a WebQuest is to provide your students with opportunities to explore content in meaningful and engaging ways.

The WebQuest should grab students' attention and take them on an interesting quest through a topic. A WebQuest can vary in length from short and concise to long and detailed. It is usually used to introduce a topic or have students tie together understanding at the end of a learning unit.

A WebQuest is not a static activity whereby students memorize facts or write a research report. Rather, it is a dynamic learning activity in which students use the Internet to access relevant and up-to-date information and then apply that information through critical thinking by synthesizing information, analyzing content, and solving problems using creative thought.

OVERVIEW

A WebQuest is an educational tool used to engage students in the process of learning and to begin using real-world data and information found on the Internet. This Web-based activity can be an introductory or concluding activity, or it can be presented as an entire unit of study. WebQuests allow students to explore and discover information through important questions, investigation of resources, collaborative groups, role playing, and presentation.

As the teacher, you create an activity that uses quality resources that help answer the engaging quest that wraps your students into a role. For example, your students can be literary critics, owners of a circus, a zoologist, or a politician running for office.

Once you identify a role for each student to play, resources are then provided to students that you reviewed and evaluated to ensure the information is reliable and provides appropriate content to help them complete their WebQuest. The students themselves are not responsible for going out onto the Internet to find quality resources; this is something you must accomplish and present to them at the start of the WebQuest activity. The main mission of your students is to investigate the task presented.

WebQuests are a perfect example of constructivist learning. As the teacher, you present a "big idea" question, and you provide appropriate resources and instructional strategies so your students can explore and discover the information to answer important questions. Rather than focusing on memorization of terms, terminology, or procedures, a structured WebQuest activity is designed to get your students thinking critically about topics and content. The following sections depict how to design a quality WebQuest activity.

FORMATTING A WEBQUEST

Like any instructional activity, there is a structure and format to follow in order to ensure learning standards and objectives are being met, appropriate strategies are used, methods and tools are utilized, and appropriate feedback and assessments are given to ensure that students are learning what is intended. The fundamental idea of a WebQuest is to provide an inquiry-learning experience that allows students to:

1. Ask questions.
2. Make hypotheses.

3. Test hypotheses.
4. Present new understanding to others.

Your goal as a teacher is to ensure that these experiences are taking place and are appropriate.

A WebQuest also provides opportunities for students to use a technology tool such as the Internet to research real-world, up-to-date data and to review current and relevant information to help solve real-world problems. Students can then place their collected data into a spreadsheet to organize the information and create a graph. They can also use a word processor to textually present their findings for others to read.

When students begin to think critically about big idea questions in the task of the WebQuest and begin using technology to analyze and evaluate information found, learning becomes meaningful and important. Your task as the teacher and designer of a WebQuest is to keep these central ideas in mind as you create your WebQuest.

Some areas to focus on are:

1. Standards and learning objectives.
2. Authentic activities and assessments.
3. Instructional strategies that encourage collaboration.
4. Opportunities for knowledge creation and exploration through discovery and exploration.
5. Resources that identify real-world data and relevant up-to-date information.
6. Technology tools and resources to enhance your big idea question.

When you design a WebQuest, the Internet is a prominent resource for your students' investigation and discovery. The Internet provides an abundance of resources and data that are up-to-date, has primary sources readily available, and is accessible. Therefore, as a teacher creating a WebQuest, you should utilize relevant data and resources found online for your students to analyze and evaluate in order to solve the proposed problem.

In the design phase, you want to carefully plan the teaching and learning strategies as well as the activities. Your responsibility is to identify quality resources and to determine what you want your students to understand. What is the big picture? Remember, the goal of a Web-Quest is not to write a research paper but instead to explore and discover content and then share this new knowledge with others through a performance. To help illustrate, the next section reviews the components of a WebQuest.

Sections of a WebQuest

There are six central sections to prepare when designing a WebQuest. Table 3.1 identifies each of these sections, as well as a Teacher's Page and Credits section. Within each section, you provide instructional strategies, quality resources, and investigative pointers in order to ensure that students collect and organize information appropriately, remain on task throughout the WebQuest, and learn and understand the material.

As in the development of any lesson, think about and provide instructional strategies that meet the needs of your students' learning styles, resources that you have reviewed and approved, and an overall structure so students can stay on task to collect and organize information appropriately and learn and understand what is intended.

As you work through these sections when designing your WebQuest, remember this is an inquiry-oriented activity that is wrapped around big idea questions as well as learning standards and objectives, and it should provide an authentic task to engage students in exploring and creating their own understanding about a topic.

A WebQuest can be of varying length. It can be a single lesson or it can be one or two days of activity or even one to two months. The Web-Quest should be presented in a Web page format. This is important so students can easily access Internet resources that you provide them.

For another view of how a WebQuest is integrated, see figure 3.1. This organization chart provides a visual representation of a WebQuest, particularly how each section is integrated to tell a story and draw the learner into the WebQuest itself.

Table 3.1. WebQuest Design Sections

Section	Description
I. Introduction	• Introduce the student to the activity. • Emphatically capture the student's attention. • Write from a student perspective. • Option to use an advanced organizer or overview to prepare the student for what is to come. • Should be short in length.
II. Task	• Must be doable and interesting. • Task allows students to learn so they will enhance their current knowledge and gather new understanding with others. • The big idea question is presented here. • Possible tasks include: • Solving a problem • Preparing and participating in a debate • Designing a product or procedure • Multimedia presentation • Article to be written
III. Process	• Provide specific steps students should take to accomplish and complete the intended task. • Specific details on groups, roles, resources, and strategies are given. • Specific handouts students will use to complete each process are made available here. • Provide this section in an ordered list, identifying the procedures that must be followed to ensure success in the WebQuest activity. • Be very specific and detailed.
IV. Evaluation	• A check sheet and/or rubric for students to review allows them to determine what is important to accomplish and understand in the WebQuest. • Identify whether the grade will be individual, group, or both.
V. Conclusion	• Provide closure to the WebQuest by providing a summary of what students accomplished and its relevancy to their overall learning. • Questions could also be posed for students to investigate further if they are interested. • This identifies learning as a continuous process.
VI. Resources	• Provide a list of resources that students can use to find necessary information. • Organize the information in categories so students can find appropriate information at a glance.
Teacher's Page	• This is the only section that is not written for the student. • Provide as much detail as possible about standards, objectives, and the WebQuest itself so another teacher can adopt your WebQuest or adapt it to his or her students.
Credits	• Provide a list of references and credits that were used in the WebQuest. • Remember to reference all images, music, recordings, and text.

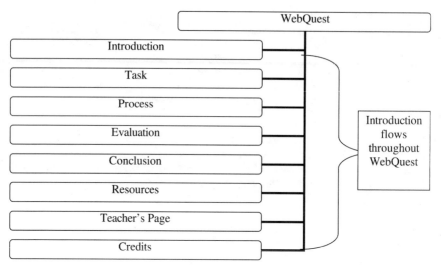

Figure 3.1. Organization of WebQuest

DESIGNING EACH SECTION OF YOUR WEBQUEST

Introduction

As with any well-constructed activity, you must first introduce the activity to the students. In the Introduction section of your WebQuest, capture your students' attention to willingly participate in the Web-Quest. Provide them with an inviting scenario that is both relevant and doable, and assign roles or introduce resources that students can explore and investigate further.

Getting your students excited about participating in the WebQuest is simple if you focus on applying a scenario or activity to their interests and experiences. For example, you can design a WebQuest so that students take a variety of roles, to include:

- A newspaper reporter investigating the story of Christopher Columbus and his Quest for India and relating Columbus's experiences to other explorers past and present.
- A mathematician investigating census data during the Civil War to identify logistics and strategic movements of the generals and the battles fought, as well as how this information influenced conflicts past and present.

- A scientist investigating the life cycle of the animal kingdom and the likely outcome if an animal or plant is removed from the life cycle.

In each of the above examples, the WebQuest draws on the interests and experiences of the students and entices them to investigate a problem or an issue that is relevant to their own history over time, their personal lives, or their community. They are playing a role and the role revolves around why the learning objective is important.

This integration with prior knowledge, personal interest, and why the topic is important to understand creates relevancy for the student and the activity itself. It also provides a connection for your students and builds on lessons learned in past activities to enhance learning in future activities.

In each example, a student should propose and test hypotheses, collect and analyze data, and then create new understandings by tying their understandings into a presentation that can be viewed and shared with others. By taking on roles or scenarios, your students are more likely to invest in the activity and have the expectation that something significant and important will occur when they reach the end of the WebQuest.

In the example of the scientist role, you could provide opportunities for your students to share their new understandings about a plant or animal taken out of the cycle of life by having an evening poster session to present the data to parents and community members and allow for a question and answer period.

Students could prepare an article for the editorial section of the local newspaper to outline their findings and new understanding and offer opportunities for the community to get more involved in life cycle issues of plants and animals from an environmental standpoint.

The Introduction does not have to stop at the first section of your WebQuest. It can be embedded throughout the WebQuest to continually provide guidance and direction for your students. For example, an expert can provide commentary throughout the WebQuest to gain each student's attention and to help and provide feedback to the student during the WebQuest. In the life cycle example, the expert can be a scientist from the Smithsonian or a parent who works at a research laboratory.

The Introduction section should provide specific details about what the WebQuest is about and what the expectations are. Its presentation should be concise so as not to overwhelm your students. Remember, you want to encourage your students to embark on this quest because it is important, and you then want to entice them to learn more and continue to the next section, the *Task*.

The "Sample Introduction" shows an example used to engage third graders studying past historic explorers. The focus of the lesson is for students to learn about the individual explorers as well as "the journey" or exploration itself. Students will study the exploration of the Americas by:

- Describing the accomplishments of Christopher Columbus, Juan Ponce de Léon, Jacques Cartier, and Christopher Newport.
- Identifying reasons for exploring, the information gained, and the results from the travels.

SAMPLE INTRODUCTION

Introduction
   Ahoy!
   Early explorers needed a lot of skills to investigate territories that were unknown and unfamiliar to them. Explorers encountered unfamiliar animals, languages, customs, foods, terrain, climates, and illnesses.
   Just as the early explorers discovered new worlds so others could learn more about the world outside of their community, so will you. Through this exploration, you will investigate the new world's environment, people, and characteristics. There is a local explorer looking for a recorder. Are you interested in the position?
   If so, go to the next section of the WebQuest, the *Task*, to begin this voyage.

The Introduction in the example is specific, engaging, and provides a relevant reason for students to continue further to the next section. Students have been introduced to both time and place as well as what their expectations will be. They are engaged and ready to go. What a great start!

Task

The next section of a WebQuest is the Task. The big question for you is, what specifically do you want your students to *do* and *accomplish*? Secondarily you want to consider how you can make the WebQuest meaningful to them personally in terms of their community, lifestyle, and/or interests.

Remember the big idea question introduced above? In this section, you want to spell it out for your students and make sure that you grab their attention. This question must be designed so that it will encourage students to think and explore the topic in depth and at a deeper level.

The idea of the Task is for your students to explore the big idea question by investigating the resources that you have provided. At the same time, your students are expected to begin slowly pulling in past information and relating this new information to an authentic context, their lives and the world at large.

Within the Task, you also provide specific expectations that you want your students to perform in order to complete the WebQuest. In order to do this, you want to provide a brief description of what you want your students to accomplish throughout the WebQuest and what performances they are expected to complete by the end of the WebQuest in your Task section.

With each section, you are building your WebQuest and slowly engaging your students into the process of working on the problem or issue you outlined. You will go into further detail in the next section, Process. Remember, each section of your WebQuest builds on the next section and slowly pulls the students deeper into the Quest itself. Designing a WebQuest is like telling a story with the final pages of the book missing.

It is during the development of the Task section that you find all your resources to help your students best complete the WebQuest. Once you have resources that provide interesting and quizzical paths for your students to explore, then it is time to begin developing the WebQuest itself. Finding the resources first helps to keep the WebQuest relevant and aligned with your standards and the overall goal of the activity.

As you create the Task section of your WebQuest, you also want to include appropriate scaffolding for each of your students in order to make the tasks manageable and doable and to encourage your students to begin the process of thinking about the content, the goals of the activity, the expectations, and each student's role in the WebQuest itself.

This can be accomplished in outline form. The goal of providing scaffolding is to ensure that a connection to prior learning is included as well as to help students develop a schema, a pattern that can continuously be called upon and reformatted when they encounter these topics and inquiry skills in future activities.

SAMPLE TASK

Task
You have just been hired by an explorer to help investigate and report on a new world. The questions that you will explore and investigate are not easy, so you will need to work in groups as you set sail on a journey across the vast ocean for the exploration.

This trip will be filled with new adventures. The explorer of this voyage needs a good reporter to keep the ship's Exploration Journal in order to record all findings and discoveries, to include people, places, cultures, foods, artifacts, and the voyage itself.

Your group will also design an Exhibit, using your Exploration Journal as a resource, to inform the community about faraway discoveries on your return and how these discoveries have impacted our lives today.

You will be divided into four different explorer groups. Each group will be assigned an explorer who will be Captain of the ship.

The explorers are:

- Christopher Columbus
- Juan Ponce de Léon
- Jacques Cartier
- Christopher Newport

As the reporter, you will be in charge of the ship's Exploration Journal and the collection of all artifacts in order to share the journey and the discoveries with others. Requirements are provided below.

In your investigation you will:

- Observe the strength of mind of the explorer.
- Document all trials and tribulations during the journey.

- List discoveries and achievements.
- Reflect on the importance of discovery and achievement in today's world.

In addition, you will note:

- New cultures, languages, customs, and products.
- Any problems encountered.
- Interesting facts that were discovered.

The Exploration Journal will be used to take notes and collect artifacts during the exploration itself. The Journal must contain the following items:

- Reason for exploration.
- Biographical information of the explorer.
- Personality of the explorer.
- Cargo and food report with images, sketches, position on ship, etc.
- Sketches or images of boats, maps, people, jewelry, foods, plants, animals, structures, etc., that were encountered and collected during the voyage.
- Navigator report.

Your Exploration Group will design an Exhibit in the appropriate theme of the new world explored, highlighting the information collected during your travels.

The Exhibit participants will be your peers, parents, and the school community.

This Exhibit can use PowerPoint, HyperStudio, images, sound clips, poster, and/or brochure to display information and content found.

Process

The Process section provides specific details about each group's role in the WebQuest as well as each individual group member's role. As suggested earlier, a WebQuest should have collaboration among students built into the WebQuest whereby each member in the group assumes a different role or perspective.

In this section, you want to cover the following specific attributes:

- Outline the goals of the WebQuest.
- Restate your interesting and engaging problem for students to explore and discover.
- Provide quality and relevant resources to help each student explore the problem in detail.
- Meaningful collaborative groups are assigned to help each student identify a specific role or perspective of the problem.

All of these attributes provide the WebQuest with a sense of relevancy and meaningful real-world experience which will aid in grabbing your students' attention and pulling them into the WebQuest.

The goal of the WebQuest is to create an activity that will engage students in the topic and content to be explored so that they can discover new information and go beyond current knowledge to develop their own understanding and then present this new understanding to others in a meaningful way. The Process section identifies and describes strategies and resources you want your students to use to complete the Task.

SAMPLE PROCESS

Process
Now let's begin our Exploration!

You and your group will be in charge of the Exploration Journal. The Exploration Journal will contain many different artifacts and written accounts of the journey itself. You will use your Journal to design and create your Exhibit.

You will be divided into groups that will investigate and go along on the exploration. Your group will be members of the crew of one of the explorers below:

- Christopher Columbus
- Juan Ponce de Léon

- Jacques Cartier
- Christopher Newport

Your teacher will give you your Ship's assignment before you begin. Through this exploration, you will collect information and be prepared as a group to share this new information with the class in an exhibit.

Why Explore?
In order to do a good job for your Captain, you must understand who he or she is. You will start by watching a short video about explorations. (Video link)

Use your Exploration Journal to list factual information about exploring that you discovered while watching the video.

Take notes on what explorations consist of. Next, what makes a good explorer?

After writing and reflecting in your Journal, we will discuss your findings as a class. During this discussion, we will identify similarities and differences of explorers and identify some key characteristics of a good explorer. During this discussion, do not forget to jot down some interesting facts in your Journal!

Now it is time to explore a couple of Web sites to learn some interesting facts about your specific explorer.

Resources:
- Why Explore?
  http://library.thinkquest.org/C001692/english/indexphp3?subject=why

Get to Know Your Explorer
It is important before we begin any exploration to learn about your Captain, the explorer. Who is this person? Who commissioned him? Why is this commission important? What do you think the personality of the explorer is?
  Resources:
- Enchanted Learning: Juan Ponce de León
  http://www.enchantedlearning.com/explorers/page/d/deleon.shtml
- Encarta: Juan Ponce de León
  http://encarta.msn.com/ ponce_de_leon.html

- History Channel: Juan Ponce de Léon
  http://www.history.com/encyclopedia.do?articleId=219594

Cargo and Food Report
As you set sail on your exploration, you must make sure that your ship's cargo list is complete. You want to make sure that the ship is fully stocked with food for your crew for this long and uncertain voyage.

Gather information about foods that were available during the time period of your explorer and design a list of items you will need for your ship.

Make sure you address such questions as:

- What will the crew drink?
- What types of fruits, vegetables, and meats will make the journey?
- Will flour be needed?
- What herbs can be used to make food tasty?
- How will food be stored?
- Will you stop along the way to get more food?
- Will you have opportunities to fish or hunt for food?
- What else will you bring on your voyage? Investigate what else your explorer might have brought with him or her by thinking about what kind of clothes were needed, what tools were needed, trading trinkets or other items you discover.

When you have your ship's Cargo and Food Report, add it to your Exploration Journal.

Resources:
Juan Ponce de Léon
- World Fact Book
  http://www.faqs.org/docs/factbook/countrylisting.html

Navigator Report
Now that you are familiar with your explorer and your ship is fully stocked, it is time to set sail. But how will the Captain know where to go? Well, as the first mate, it is your job to make sure the Captain is able to reach the destination.

First, you will determine how explorers navigated their ships during this time period and report your findings so that the Captain can be prepared when you set sail.

Second, you will design and create a map of the journey the explorer took to reach his destination. You will need to print out a world map that shows where your explorer began and the route he took to his final destination. (*World Map worksheet*) Make sure that you label your map with the following information:

- Country where the explorer started his or her voyage.
- Country where the voyage ended.
- The body of water traveled across.
- The equator and different hemispheres.

Draw a navigational symbol showing North, South, East, and West

Resources:
Juan Ponce de Léon
- Encarta: Ponce de Léon exploration map
  http://encarta.msn.com/media_461517666/Early_European_
  Explorers.html

Finally, draw a picture of the ship and what it must have looked like when it landed at the destination. Don't forget to take note of such things as wildlife or rivers in your drawing.

Add all these items to your Exploration Journal.

Achievements of Explorer Report
Land Ahoy!
You have safely made it to your destination!

Now as the first mate, it is your responsibility to continue to write notes in your Explorer's Journal in order to keep an accurate and up-to-date report for everyone in your homeland. Make sure to log, in your Exploration Journal, information that will be relevant for your Exhibit, such as:

- Where did you land?
- What was found?

- Were there any native people? If so, who were they? What was interesting about them? What was similar? Identify who they are and what they are like.
- Are there raw materials to build homes or survive? What kind of homes might you build?
- What types of plants are there to eat? Should seeds be sent over on future voyages? If so, what types of seed would be best for the climate and terrain?
- What kind of wildlife is there?
- Is this the final destination of the explorer or does the explorer set sail soon afterward and explore further?

Everyone at home is very curious, so your Exploration Journal must be very detailed. It should tell of your adventure and the discovery of this new land and what it has to offer.

Don't forget to include in your Exploration Journal at least two drawings of interesting artifacts so everyone at home can see what this new land and people look like.

Resources:
Juan Ponce de Léon
- Social Studies for Kids: Juan Ponce de Léon
  http://www.socialstudiesforkids.com/articles/worldhistory/juanponcedeleon1.htm

*Note: This Process is only a fragment of the Process section, as only limited resources and information were provided to this illustration. In your actual Process section, more relevant and useful resources and text would need to be provided so students do not have to struggle to find information. Be specific with your resources.

Evaluation

In an inquiry-oriented activity such as a WebQuest, students should be aware from the very beginning how they are going to be evaluated. What are the expectations of this WebQuest and what is important for them to understand? To do this, you want to design a rubric that identifies your learning objectives and is easy for your students to follow and comprehend.

You may want to highlight Benjamin Bloom's taxonomy of application, synthesis, and evaluation to ensure that students are thinking critically about the task at hand. An authentic evaluation tool such as a rubric is the best method to use with a WebQuest.

When students review the rubric, they are able to determine what is expected of them throughout the WebQuest activity. Specific criteria are required for success. The student will see that the value 4 is exemplary, but it also allows students to go above and beyond, achieving a value of 5 if they demonstrate exceptionally outstanding effort.

The rubric also allows group members to evaluate each other. Table 3.2 shows a complete and well-rounded rubric that will keep students on task and focused throughout the WebQuest. The most important thing about using a rubric as an evaluation and assessment tool is that it be relevant, consistent, and fair.

Conclusion

The conclusion of a WebQuest provides a summary of the activity, congratulations to your students for completing the WebQuest, and questions for further investigation.

SAMPLE CONCLUSION

Conclusion
Your explorer cannot thank you enough for all your attention to detail in the ship's Exploration Journal. The King and Queen also thank you for the detailed letter and drawings of the newly discovered land.

It is time to share your Exploration Journal with your classmates!

What does it suggest to say that someone is an explorer?
How do explorations impact others' lives?
Are there any present-day explorers?

Table 3.2. Evaluation Example

Category	Above and Beyond 5	Exemplary 4	Accomplished 3	Developing 2	Beginning 1	Score (1, 2, 3, 4, or 5)
What did you learn about your explorer and the exploration itself?	Identified and listed more than 7 findings and artifacts. Wrote more than 4 sentences without errors and with excellent sentence structure.	Identified and listed 7 or more findings and artifacts. Wrote 4 or more sentences without errors and with excellent sentence structure.	Identified and listed 4 or more findings and artifacts. Wrote sentences with good sentence structure and few errors.	Identified and listed 3 or 4 findings and artifacts. Wrote 2 or 3 sentences with several errors.	Identified and listed 2 or 3 findings and artifacts. Wrote 1 or 2 sentences without sentence structure.	
Completed task for exploration.	Completed each step within the process and gathered evidence. No grammatical errors.	Completed all areas without grammatical errors.	Completed 4 or 5 areas with few grammatical errors.	Completed 3 or 4 areas with several grammatical errors.	Completed 2 areas with many grammatical errors.	

Ecosystem scavenger hunt.	Identified all 7 aspects and was able to explain why each was important to another part of the ecosystem.	Found all 7 aspects and could explain why each was important to the ecosystem.	Found 5 to 7 aspects and could explain why several were important to the ecosystem.	Found 3 to 5 aspects and could explain why a couple were important to the ecosystem.	Found 1 to 3 aspects and could not articulate why any were important to the ecosystem.
Diagram of your type of farm.	Achieved exemplary level then included ideas to enhance the farming experience.	Detailed drawing of farm includes all aspects of farm ecosystem. Color and extras added.	Drawing of farm with 3 or more aspects of farm ecosystem. Color and an extra added.	Drawing of farm. May include aspect of ecosystem. May include color but limited effort.	Drawing of farm. Does not include aspect of ecosystem. Little color, little effort.
Commercial	Achieved exemplary level and included props, costumes, etc.	Included an identifiable jingle, humor, and many aspects they learned about their type of farm. Outstanding effort.	Included jingle, some humor, and several aspects about their type of farm. Could engage audience more.	Included jingle, little humor, and one or two aspects about the farm. Lacks enthusiasm.	May include jingle and little humor. May include aspects about farm. Minimal effort.

Resources

In the Resources section, you want to provide a list of all resources that students will use to complete the WebQuest Task. This list should be easily accessible and readable. These same resources are also in the Process section of your WebQuest.

The reason you also put them in this section is for easy access. You do not want students to become confused or frustrated while completing the WebQuest activity. Instead, you want them to remain focused on achieving the goal of the lesson.

The resources that you use for your WebQuest will primarily come from the Internet. You can use a variety of resources as long as they are relevant. Resources can include video, sound files, maps, experts, graphics, manipulatives, models, and images. Any resource can be used that allows students to think about each element within their task and motivates them to continue with the WebQuest.

SAMPLE RESOURCES

Resources:
Juan Ponce de Léon
  • Enchanted Learning: Juan Ponce de Léon
    http://www.enchantedlearning.com/explorers/page/d/deleon.shtml
  • Encarta: Juan Ponce de Léon
    http://encarta.msn.com/ ponce_de_leon.html
  • History Channel: Juan Ponce de Léon
    http://www.history.com/encyclopedia.do?articleId=219594

Teacher's Page

In this section, you want to provide information for other teachers who may be interested in adopting your WebQuest. Provide them with all the information they will need to implement your activity successfully. Standards of learning and technology standards covered should be clearly identified.

Also, provide your big idea question, resources that you utilized throughout your WebQuest, and teaching strategies implemented. In addition, identify any problems that a teacher may encounter with a specific resource or strategy.

You may also want to identify any supplies or resources that are necessary to complete this WebQuest. It is also helpful to include a note regarding any changes made since your last revision (if applicable) or ideas for extensions with specific students. You may additionally request that teachers who have used your WebQuest contact you regarding what worked best and what could be improved upon. The more detailed you are on the Teacher's Page the better.

A sampling of scaffolding activities that teachers may implement to prepare students for the WebQuest should also be provided. Outline each activity that the groups work through to complete the WebQuest. The most important focus of this section is to prepare prospective users of your WebQuest before they begin implementing the WebQuest with their students in their classrooms. What do you want them to know?

You can provide links to relevant pages of your WebQuest to help teachers see and review what your expectations are for the WebQuest. Remember, this is an interactive Web document, so using hyperlinks to areas within your WebQuest is very appropriate and useful.

SAMPLE TEACHER'S PAGE

Teacher's Page
- Background of WebQuest standards of learning
- Content
- Technology
- Notes and important information about this WebQuest
- Teaching strategies and methods
- Resources used
- Possible resources to add to the WebQuest
- Further reading about the topic
- Contact me (Feedback)

Credits

Make sure to formally cite all sources used in your WebQuest in the Credits section. This includes images, video, and text. Citing sources is important to model good Internet behavior to your students. In this section, you also want to list all resources used throughout your WebQuest to provide easy access to your students.

As discussed above, you can create a WebQuest that is engaging, interesting, and fun and at the same time that provides opportunities for students to explore and discover information and then present this new information to a larger audience. As illustrated, this is not a static research project or an activity to have students memorize terms and terminology. The Sample WebQuest Template can also serve as a guide to help you get started.

SAMPLE WEBQUEST TEMPLATE

WebQuest Template
Title of the Lesson
A WebQuest for <u>xth</u> Grade for <u>Content Area</u>
Designed by _____
Contact Information _____
Graphic that highlights task, content, or subject

Introduction | Task | Process | Evaluation | Conclusion | Resources | Teacher's Page | Credits

Introduction
Introduce the student to the activity and emphatically capture the students' attention. Prepare your WebQuest with your students in mind. Use an advanced organizer or overview to prepare the student for what is to come. The introduction should be short in length.

Task
Must be doable and interesting and allow the students to advance their understanding of the information they have gathered in order to share their newly acquired information with others. This is where you place your "big idea" question. Some possible tasks could include:

- Solve a problem.
- Prepare and participate in a debate.
- Design a product or procedure.
- Multimedia presentation.
- Article to be written.

Process
Provide specific steps that students will take and accomplish to complete the intended task. Specific details on groups, roles, resources, and strategies are given. Specific handouts that students use to complete each process are provided. This section is organized in an ordered list, identifying the procedures that must be followed to ensure success in the WebQuest. Make certain that your presentation is very specific and detailed.

Evaluation
Provide a check sheet and/or rubric for students to review in order to determine what is important for them to accomplish and understand in the WebQuest. Identify whether their grade will be individual, group, or both.

Conclusion
Provide closure to the WebQuest itself by providing a summary of what students accomplished and its relevancy to their overall learning. You could also pose questions for students to investigate further. This identifies learning as a continuous process.

Resources
A list of resources should be provided that students can review to find information. The resources should be organized into categories so that the information is easy to access.

Teacher's Page
Provide as much detail as possible about standards, objectives, and the WebQuest itself so that another teacher can adopt your WebQuest.

Credits
Provide a list of references and credits that you used in your WebQuest. Reference all images, music, recordings, and text. Also, if you used other resources such as books or people, you would list them in this section.

SUMMARY

In a WebQuest, students work in collaborative groups on a relevant topic that aligns with your learning standards, and at the same time they are encouraged to further explore the material in more detail.

The design of your WebQuest is very important. Since this is a WebQuest that will be located on the Web, you want to think about interactivity, graphics and fonts used, as well as your use of colors to help engage students in the WebQuest itself.

Overall, a WebQuest provides information to students. Students think critically about this information and then present it to others as a group. Your goal as a teacher is to provide quality information and effective learning strategies in order to get students thinking and creating new knowledge. Students should not be passively working through your WebQuest. Instead, they should be talking, debating, discussing, sharing, analyzing, and critiquing information and ideas.

FURTHER INVESTIGATION

Best WebQuests. http://www.bestWebQuests.com/.
Dodge, B.: A Rubric for Evaluating WebQuests. http://WebQuest.sdsu.edu/WebQuestrubric.html.
Filimentality Web-based Activity Tool. http://www.kn.att.com/wired/fil/.
Idea Generator. http://tommarch.com/learning/idea_machine.php.
Spartanburg: WebQuest Evaluation Form. http://www.spa3.k12.sc.us/WebQuestrubric.htm.
Student Process Guides. http://projects.edtech.sandi.net/staffdev/tpss99/processguides/index.htm.
WebQuest Generator. http://www.bestteachersites.com/web_tools/web_quest/.
WebQuest Page. http://WebQuest.org/index.php.
What Are WebQuests Really? By Tom Marsh. http://bestWebQuests.com/what_WebQuests_are.asp.

REFLECTION

1. Summarize three main goals of a WebQuest.
2. What makes a WebQuest an inquiry-oriented activity?

3. Why is it important for a big idea question to drive a WebQuest?
4. When designing a WebQuest, it is best to provide relevant and quality resources for students to use. Explain why this is so important.

SKILL-BUILDING ACTIVITY

Throughout this chapter, we explored how to create a WebQuest using the Internet. The focus was on engaging your students in an interesting and doable activity so that they are motivated to think, explore, and discover new information. Your goal now is to create a WebQuest that aligns with your learning standards, is developed around an interesting and doable big idea question, uses quality resources, and provides opportunities for students to complete a meaningful presentation of their new knowledge.

4

CREATING A WEB INQUIRY ACTIVITY

A Web inquiry activity uses the unfiltered Web to encourage your students to explore and investigate information. Raw resources such as primary source documents, book reviews, and data are accessed by students so they can ask questions, explore content, and determine possible results. One reason Web inquiry is beneficial is the opportunity for questions to be tied both to standards of learning and real-life events, problems, resources, and data.

As Benjamin Bloom's taxonomy suggests, teachers should move their students from memorization to higher-level investigation and thinking. This is done by creating activities that provide opportunities for students to synthesize and analyze information in order for them to begin thinking critically about questions posed in all situations and to then develop questions on their own. Ultimately, you want them to do this with unfiltered information to provide a real-world approach to learning.

OVERVIEW

A Web inquiry activity revolves around good open-ended questions tied around learning standards. When you have found learning standards that highlight inquiry, you can begin writing your objectives. How do you want students to demonstrate their understanding of these standards, and what will your students produce when they complete this activity?

Because this is a Web inquiry activity, good online data are required. Students find data that use real-time databases or primary source documents and then they are able to utilize this timely, meaningful, and raw data to help answer questions. This allows students to explore an open-ended question that you provided them in an unfiltered way. In other words, no one has interpreted these data for them, like a textbook author. When students look at raw data, they must critically think about the information to find possible solutions.

The purpose of a Web inquiry activity is to provide your students with meaningful opportunities to use raw data—data that have not been filtered—so they can both manipulate and interpret data to create meaning and sift through and discover possible solutions.

For example, you can have students explore global warming on many different levels. Students can be placed into collaborative groups to explore specific elements of this broad issue. In one group, for example, students can explore a question about alternative energy sources, both the benefits and shortcomings.

One database that students can draw data from could be the commodity stock exchange for live data. Questions could be posed such as:

- How has the price of corn changed over the past five years?
- What have been some of the benefits of this price change?
- What have been some of the drawbacks of this price change?
- How do these changes impact the environment?

A WebQuest is similar to a Web inquiry activity because it uses information primarily from the Web, except a WebQuest contains resources for students to explore chosen by you, the teacher. A Web inquiry activity is designed to give guidance to the teacher but not necessarily the student. Rather, this is true scientific inquiry such that the inquiry activity provides little information and guidance, in order for the student to investigate, discover, and ultimately make predictions. Maximum flexibility is given to the student to encourage creativity in completing a Web inquiry activity.

The only part of a Web inquiry activity that you provide to your students is the first section, the part called the "Hook." Remember, the idea is to provide as little information as possible to your students in order to enhance the inquiry elements of the activity itself.

It is important to note that your role in this process is to guide your students throughout the inquiry activity by asking questions and guiding them to appropriate resources that will help them find answers to important questions.

INQUIRY USING THE INTERNET

The best Web inquiry activity starts with an open-ended question. Open-ended questions do not identify a solution, and because of this, your students are compelled to explore many possibilities or hypotheses in order to discover a good meaning or solution to the overall problem.

For example, for a science unit on the theme of global warming, the open-ended question could focus on how human consumption and production impact the rising global climate. To answer this question, students would use their prior understandings of climate, consumption, and production and then begin identifying what information they need to best answer this question.

Students would begin researching a variety of data sources, such as weather data, government records and reports, and production rates of goods and services. Students would then take this new information and combine it in a white paper that they could then submit to local community leaders.

Web inquiry activities provide good Web resources that give your students opportunities to collect and discover information, such as raw data sites or the U.S. Census Bureau at http://www.census.gov/schools/facts/, in order to collect data over time for population growth in specific parts of the country. This helps answer questions about the possibilities of global warming as it relates to population growth in urban and rural areas.

A good Web inquiry activity focuses on either guided inquiry or open inquiry. In guided inquiry, the teacher *guides* the process of student inquiry, either by providing resources and/or asking leading questions. A guided inquiry could be used to introduce students to the process of inquiry. This is not a natural skill. All of us must be taught how to develop questions, answer questions, create hypotheses, and make predictions. How do we look critically at information to make good decisions?

The other inquiry process is open inquiry. Here an open-ended question is posed by the teacher to students. Instead of guiding the discovery process of the student, the teacher *facilitates* the process and allows students to take the lead role in the discovery and investigative process. The teacher therefore facilitates the process to ensure that students are on task, are productive, and are learning what is important and intended.

Regardless of which inquiry method you choose, guided or open, an inquiry activity has the potential to provide an authentic learning experience to your students. Your students then are able to practice critical thinking in order to build the Web inquiry activity around an authentic problem.

This elicits student interest in the topic and helps them discover relevancy to the content itself. How many times have you heard "Why do I need to know this?" Through this authentic Web inquiry activity, questions such as this are answered.

Guidelines in any activity are important and there is no exception when it comes to a Web inquiry-oriented activity. Whether you are using guided or open inquiry the need for guidelines applies. Your students need structure or they will get lost throughout the process, and then learning on the intended objectives will not occur. Your focus when designing a Web inquiry activity is to include structure in the activity itself.

Traditional inquiry activities usually revolved around set answers or solutions. Students typically practiced inquiry skills but each activity completed had a specific answer. Resources provided and used by students came primarily through textbooks. Even science experiments usually had prescribed outcomes.

As teachers involved in twenty-first-century teaching and learning, we now have the potential to have our students access live information and manipulate raw data in order for them to question information and tie information into their own understanding. In order for this to happen, you as the teacher must pose good questions and use relevant and timely resources to help your students build inquiry skills.

A Web inquiry activity is both a hands-on and minds-on activity from the perspective of both the teacher and the students. As the teacher, you must actively participate in the activity with your students by asking questions and helping to guide them through the inquiry process. This active participation from you provides your students with continued opportunities to test their theories and assumptions in order to answer questions.

For students to be successfully engaged, the teacher must provide a variety of learning strategies, such as visual mind maps, small and large collaborative groups, think-pair-share, and opportunities for discussion, reflection, and feedback. Each strategy used must help your students scaffold new understandings.

One major benefit of a Web inquiry activity is this constant connection with your students to ensure that good questions are being asked and answered. If the idea is to provide an activity that allows your students to sit quietly at their computers to work on a solo activity, a Web inquiry activity is not the activity to choose. A Web inquiry activity is an interactive exercise.

WHY WEB INQUIRY?

The Internet provides its users with many different sources of information. This information can come in the form of primary source documents, raw data, and newspapers, journals, blogs, Wikis, images, and video. Each source provides an opportunity for your students to gather resources and then to manipulate the information to answer important questions and to create new meaning.

Data obtained from the Internet are both quantitative and qualitative in nature. There may be news reports, studies, personal reflections, and raw facts and figures maintained by governments and organizations.

This use of unfiltered information allows students to organize and decipher the resources to aid in answering important questions. This is how an economist makes decisions in his or her daily job, by taking raw data and manipulating the material in order to answer specific questions.

This process is a good example of thinking critically about topics that are relevant to us, both inside and outside the classroom. A student could study economics by reading the textbook about ideas involving the gross national product and the consumer price index to learn about how both of these concepts impact the nation's economy, or that student can go to the Department of Labor's Web site at http://www.dol.gov/dol/audience/aud-students.htm to find actual data that the economists are reviewing to make decisions. This real-world application helps to create meaning and validity for the student regarding these economic concepts.

This real-world approach provides a different learning experience for students. When you have guided or open inquiry using the Internet as a resource, your students have opportunities to experience and discover learning. This is a very powerful learning opportunity.

When the Internet was initially introduced into our schools, it was used as a traditional research tool. Instead of students going into the library, searching the card catalog, and choosing a book from the shelf, they now go to a search engine such as Google and type in random key words in the hopes of finding something they can use for information on their report. This type of Internet project does not involve discovery or investigation.

Inquiry is asking questions and then critically evaluating resources to determine if they are accurate, credible, and help to solve the overall problem. As new resources are found, more questions are asked. The benefit of the Internet in this process is the availability of online databases. Online databases are unfiltered and contain raw data from government sites, primary source documents housed at universities, even the Library of Congress American Memory Project found at http://memory.loc.gov.

How is Web inquiry different from using a textbook or a book from the library? The difference is the raw unfiltered data. Using raw data provides the students with unfiltered information, thereby allowing them to ask questions and determine for themselves the best possible answers to the problem.

Importantly, instead of having the answer interpreted from someone else and then presented to your students, they now additionally have the opportunity to use the Internet to discover and explore information and create their own interpretations, connections, and meanings. At the same time, students are learning important research skills through real-world experiences.

For example, suppose you had a unit to have your students learn about presidents and their role in the history of the United States. You could have your students read their textbook about the role each president played in history, or you could have students access the American Memory Project at the Library of Congress to explore primary source documents of each of the presidents, such as letters from Thomas Jefferson and Abraham Lincoln, to not only learn about their policies but also discover their feelings and intentions. The open-ended question therefore centers on asking students why presidents did what they did and how their actions impacted their community and the world at large.

In today's "flat" world, we need to provide opportunities for students that require them to think and move away from transcribing, summarizing, and reformatting information that they collect. Instead, they need to move toward using information to make decisions, ask questions, create, and present this new knowledge in meaningful ways for others to learn from and explore.

WHAT IS WEB INQUIRY?

A Web inquiry activity is a good strategy for incorporating the Internet into the curriculum. It provides structure and specific guidelines to ensure that teachers stay focused on student learning and discovery. At the same time, it teaches students good inquiry skills, such as questioning and finding good information to make informed decisions.

This type of activity provides a student-centered approach, giving students the opportunity to take the lead role in this process. It also contains elements of constructivism where your students can construct meaning. Although Web inquiry activities are designed to provide more control to your students, the teacher must play an active role by facilitating and guiding the learning process. You do this by providing scaffolding activities to ensure that your students are on task and are asking good questions, finding good resources, and creating good insights about the topics that are being explored.

For example, if students are studying the Civil War in the United States, they typically read history books to discover what the conflict was about and the results of the war. Little is understood about the personal conflicts of war among families, neighbors, and communities. The study of the Civil War could involve each of these elements by including primary source documents, from the Library of Congress, such as letters from soldiers to their family members. This would help to answer an open-ended and big idea question such as how the Civil War impacted families and communities.

Census data obtained during that period could also be accessed to determine who lived in these communities. Newspaper articles could be accessed to determine the news of the cities and towns during that time period. Each would provide information and allow students to identify answers to their questions about this time in history and how the Civil War impacted the United States.

PLANNING FOR INQUIRY

When teachers begin thinking about a Web inquiry activity they should consider a few elements. These elements are as follows:

1. Identify an open-ended question to ask students that aligns with your learning standards and objectives.
2. Identify Internet resources that will provide students with the most complete way to answer the posed question. You should try to find raw data, primary sources, and library databases.
3. Identify learning strategies students can use to manipulate the data obtained to best answer the posed question. Small-group work, using a spreadsheet to organize, compute, and display data, or interviewing community members to collect primary data are some examples.
4. Identify possible answers to the open-ended question using a variety of sources and then present this new information to others using the Internet, presentation software, or multimedia.

As you can see from the list above, you should have a clear and defined plan in order to guide your students down the path of inquiry. Lessons must be well defined or the intended goal of the lesson will be lost. You want to create an activity that piques students' curiosity and encourages them to investigate further.

As you identify important open-ended questions to help focus your activity, the next step is to identify and determine the process of inquiry that you want your students to take. Throughout these steps, you want your students to reflect on the information gathered and how this new information helps or hinders solving the proposed problem.

Throughout this inquiry process, your students reflect on the proposed question and then begin to ask questions, identify procedures to help answer the proposed question, gather and investigate data, analyze and manipulate data, and then present their findings for others to use and learn from. Figure 4.1 identifies the process your students should follow during your Web inquiry activity.

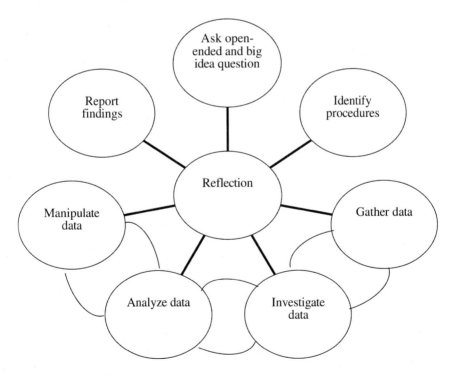

Figure 4.1.   Inquiry Process

DESIGNING A GOOD WEB INQUIRY

The main idea of a Web inquiry activity is for students to work with and manipulate information to create new understandings. Within this activity, teachers are not giving information to students; instead, they are providing a structured opportunity for students to work with all types of information, such as numbers, text, images, sounds, and video. This is the type of information that they must become familiar and work directly with. We want our students to think, question, and explore.

A Web inquiry activity is a good tool for providing students with a variety of information that they then manipulate and think about. But even if you have identified a good open-ended question and provided a variety of data types, you must identify and align both with your learning goal. You must determine what is important for your students to understand about the topic. Table 4.1 provides an example of what you should think about to organize your thoughts around designing a good inquiry activity.

The outline is broken down into four specific questions:

1. Why is this problem important? How does it relate to the real world?
2. What information needs to be collected to best answer this problem?
3. What must students understand from this problem?
4. How can this new knowledge be presented so others can learn from it?

When designing a Web inquiry activity, you must begin by thinking and planning for what is important and why it is important for your students to understand. You need to create an open-ended question that aligns with your learning objectives and engages your students to remain on task. One way to do this is to break down your learning goal into questions that you can design your activity around, such as the four questions shown above.

A Web inquiry activity is different from a WebQuest. In a WebQuest, you are creating a structured inquiry-oriented activity that provides Web resources at specific points throughout the WebQuest to help your

Table 4.1. Organizing Thoughts around a Web Inquiry Activity

Questions about the Overall Task	How to Accomplish
• Why is this question important in the real world?	*Impact:* Geography, anthropology, and sociology. *Problem statement:* A company is sending employees to another region of the world. Employees must know the culture and environment in order to best prepare for this relocation.
• What type of information is needed? • What is the best way to present information to employees easily and efficiently?	*Type:* Map of region and information on place in the world. Explore Web sites from the region and surrounding regions to gather data about culture, weather, and topography: • Google Earth • CIA Fact Book • United Nations *Present information:* Develop a brochure to provide important facts about laws, culture, customs, environment, and language.
• What do you want your students to understand?	Differences and similarities in culture, customs, language, and geographic environment.
• What specific tools and information will be needed to ensure that the correct information is gathered and new knowledge obtained?	Students can utilize facts, figures, pictures, video clips, personal Web sites, country Web sites, and government Web sites, and use presentation software.

Activity:
Students work in small groups to gather necessary and important information about Afghanistan, such as its customs, environment, industries, foods, language, and culture, in order to provide a guide to employees who are transferring to the country to help rebuild the infrastructure.
Evaluation:
A rubric that includes criteria that cover the quality of data identified and how the data help solve the problem. The rubric will also provide criteria that cover presentation quality and effectiveness.

Time frame to complete this activity: Two 50-minute class periods.

students complete the task. You want to assign your students to specific roles that provide them with a real-world problem and ensure that they are provided with outlined procedures to follow in order to complete the task effectively and efficiently.

It is possible for a WebQuest to be completed independently by the student because the quest itself is organized throughout with resources, a specific task, and well-identified procedures that provide scaffolding throughout the process. A Web inquiry activity is intended to be a guided discovery with the teacher being directly involved in order to scaffold the student throughout the process of investigation. A Web inquiry activity is intended to be completed in small groups.

DESIGNING A WEB INQUIRY ACTIVITY

In this section, the six parts that must be considered when designing a Web inquiry activity are explored:

1. The Hook that grabs your students' attention.
2. Getting students to identify other questions.
3. Procedures to guide students through the process of inquiry.
4. Exploration of data.
5. Analyzing data.
6. Presenting findings.

THE HOOK

This is the only section that your students see. The Hook is the open-ended, big idea question that grabs their attention and takes them into the problem to be explored and discovered. This is where you provide your students the topical question. They take this question and as a group begin identifying subquestions. The topical question should engage the students in the task and most importantly spark their interest.

In this section, you want students to identify key areas within the topical question and begin reflecting on the question. You do this as a class to spark interest, identify prior knowledge, and highlight key and important points to focus on during the process of inquiry. Your role as the teacher during the Hook stage is to:

- Encourage students to reflect on prior knowledge.
- Interest them in the new material that is coming.

- Provide the Hook (the open-ended question).
- Provide supporting ideas and resources for the initial Hook question.
- Have students start moving forward with the activity.

The Hook is the initial phase in the activity that grabs student interest. This is the section of the activity that students see. It is important to include a question that is relevant to your curriculum and which ties into your students' interests. The Hook should grab the students' attention to begin their investigation. It must be engaging, structured, and open ended. Since this is the only part of the activity that students see, make it good.

SAMPLE SCENARIO

Over the past five years, the world has experienced many weather-related turbulences that have impacted human life. If you turn on any news channel or read any newspaper headline, there are discussions about the threat of global warming. There is significant controversy over the issue of human consumption and global warming, both among scientists and politicians. Questions such as the following are continually debated:

- Is this because of politics and policy, or is global warming really occurring and is human consumption a portion of its cause?
- Is there a relationship among CO_2 emissions and the warming of the planet Earth?

The right questions need to be asked in order to find the right answers. It is your job to discover the truth. Therefore, consider the following:

- Is human consumption of resources causing global warming?
- Is there a relationship or an explanation between global warming and CO_2 emissions?
- Is the tremendous growth and use of resources in China having an impact on our climate?
- Are gas-guzzling SUVs playing a role?

Findings

In order for your responses and findings on the above questions to be meaningful, they must be well supported. Consider tracking the following data:

- temperature
- weather patterns and disturbances
- topography
- population
- automobile statistics over a 10-year time period

Remember, there may not be definitive answers to the questions that you ask.

✿ ✿ ✿

Main open-ended question (the Hook):

How much has temperature increased over the last 10 years around the globe?
How fast are temperatures increasing?

Possible subquestions:

- What weather disturbances have occurred over the past 10 years around the globe? What has been their frequency? What has been their intensity?
- Based on the data collected, can you predict what will happen in the next 10 years to climate around the world?
- Can you identify any human behavior changes that will need to occur as they relate to the global climate?
- Based on your findings, what will happen to the topography and population in the next 10, 20, and 30 years?

OTHER QUESTIONS

As students become pulled into the initial question that you provided to them, their interest in the activity grows and they become hooked. Your role is to provide students with opportunities to draw on their prior knowledge and to encourage students to begin the process of asking deeper questions of your topical question in order to begin making predictions about the topic being explored.

Many strategies can be used to begin this process. Brainstorming possible questions as a group and then having students make predictions is one way to start this initial grab and to ensure that students are pulling in their prior knowledge of the topic. You can write all their questions on the board. This way, there is a record, and similarities and differences can be identified for further investigation.

In the question section, you want to make sure that questions posed and predictions made by the students relate to the overall goal of the activity. Keep students focused. The importance of this section is to grab the students' attention and have them identify questions that help them answer your topical question.

It is a good idea for you to have handy possible questions to help guide your students down the path of inquiry. Inquiry is learned and your role in this process is to ensure that your students begin thinking about the topic and try out new ideas. In a nutshell, you are teaching your students to think.

As students begin asking questions, they should also begin finding answers, which in turn lead to new questions. This is the inquiry cycle in action.

For example, the data the students found indicate that temperatures have been steadily rising over the past 10 years in the Arctic by 2 degrees Celsius. Follow-up, new questions become:

- Do you think temperatures in other parts of the world will follow this same trend?
- What possible temperature changes do you think will be represented in different parts of the world?
- Have consumers influenced this trend in rising temperatures?

PROCEDURES TO GUIDE STUDENTS
THROUGH THE PROCESS OF INQUIRY

Once the topical question has been given, the students have asked deeper questions, and predictions have been made, it is now time for you to provide your students with specific steps and strategies to accomplish the task to order to solve the problem. To do this, you need answers for each of the following questions:

- What do you want your students to understand?
- How will students understand this topic?
- What types of data are required?
- How will students demonstrate to others the new knowledge they have gained from this activity?

At this stage of the Web inquiry process, the teacher's role is to continue to provide guidance by designing an activity that focuses on inquiry, good resources, and presentation of new knowledge.

Once students have asked questions about the topic and pulled from the topic possible solutions, they need to determine which steps they will need to take to find the best possible answers.

STEPS TO FIND THE INFORMATION NEEDED

1. What types of data will I need to find the answers to my questions?
2. What terms do I need to define to better understand them?
3. What types of tools will be needed to manipulate my data?
4. How will I present my manipulated data in order to share the information with others?

Types of Data
- national world temperature data
- influence of temperatures on global weather patterns
- consumer spending and world temperatures

Defining Important Terms
- global warming
- statistical analysis
- graphs

Resources
- Regional Climate Centers. http://met-www.cit.cornell.edu/other_rcc.html
- National Oceanographic Data Center. http://www.nodc.noaa.gov/
- NSF Geosciences Integrated Earth Information Server (IEIS). http://atm.geo.nsf.gov/

Tools to Manipulate Data
- spreadsheet
- math
- graphs
- databases

EXPLORATION OF DATA

Students use information obtained from the Internet to investigate your topical question and subquestions. You are preparing your students to find reliable and relevant information and ensuring that the information they are finding is helping them to answer the questions. It is important to let students find the resources but to be available with additional resources that they can use if they run into problems.

During this stage, the students investigate and explore online information in the attempt to answer the intended questions. The teacher assists to ensure that the information obtained and reported is accurate and credible.

ANALYZING DATA

In this section, students manipulate the found data in order to create new knowledge. For example, students collect census data to determine changes in the population over the past 10 years. Students can put the raw data into a spreadsheet to manipulate and then can draw meaningful conclusions from this new information created.

It is important that needed tools are available for students to use as appropriate. For example, if students are looking at textual data, they may need to organize and store the information in a database in order to conduct inquiries to answer important questions. It is also a good idea to provide examples to students on how to manipulate specific types of data in order to help answer their identified questions. This helps them to understand both the process and why this process of data manipulation is important in solving the intended problem.

Data are placed in a spreadsheet to manipulate. The development of graphs, trend lines, and equations aids in this exploration.

URLs provided:

- weather database
- consumer database
- global warming studies

Web sites provide raw numerical data as well as graphs representing temperature changes over time. Students need to transfer data found into their spreadsheet in order to analyze the information further and create their own graphs. Students also need to eliminate any data that are not necessary.

PRESENTATION OF FINDINGS

In the presentation of findings section, you want students to communicate with classmates and ultimately the community at large their new findings. This helps to provide relevancy to the activity. Up to this point, students have worked through a structured process of research by questioning, gathering data, reflecting on that data, manipulating the data, and analyzing the data, and now it is time for them to share their findings with others. During this section, you want students to present, discuss, and defend their results with their classmates and you, the teacher.

It is possible during this section that more questions will be identified, which will open opportunities for further inquiry. Through this process, you are teaching your students to solve problems using resources found on the Internet by using a guiding topical question and providing opportunities for your students to discover, reflect, investigate, and discuss.

WEB INQUIRY TEMPLATES

A Web inquiry template creates a teacher page that outlines the important topical questions and identifies the procedures and the specific strategies your students will use during the Web inquiry activity. A student page can also be created that identifies the Hook and provides the necessary topical questions, possible resources, and guidance for the inquiry process.

Sample Teacher Template

The Hook
Identify an interesting topic that allows your students to investigate and explore using Internet resources. The topic must interest them so they ask questions, identify procedures, and conduct a thorough investigation of the problem. This is the only section that students will see.

Identify Questions
Students are responsible for asking further and deeper questions in order to better research their topic, but you must also be prepared for this. In this section, list specific focus areas and possible questions. When students run into problems you will use these questions to probe and help direct them. You want to make sure your students remain on task and are focused.

Possible Questions

_____
_____
_____
_____
_____

You might also want to include possible subquestions that you want to ensure are asked. List them here.

_____
_____
_____
_____
_____

Your role is to be the "guide on the side." Your responsibility is to help students through this process; they should be taking the lead.

Identify Good Procedures

Again, this is what your students should be focusing on, but you should be prepared to offer assistance if needed. You want your students to have a good inquiry. Here they identify terms, resources, and tools. You can have a list to help guide your students through this process if you think it will help keep them organized.

Data Investigation

Students will explore raw unfiltered data. This means that they need to decide what is relevant and what is not. They need to determine how they will transfer the data found into a tool that will help them pull it apart and identify key elements from it. You might need to provide some guidance for your students.

You should have a list of Web sites and tools for students to use. You should keep students focused on the questions to help determine what data are needed.

Analysis

Raw data must be manipulated before the information can be used to answer identified questions. You may need to provide examples on how students can manipulate their found data to help answer their questions.

Data can be manipulated by using Excel or mind-mapping tools.

Findings

Consider how you want your students to present their findings to others. Results may not be possible, but findings should be well supported from information gathered.

In this section, students may have no clear-cut answers, but they should have identified further investigations and questions. They should list them in their presentation. This begins the inquiry cycle all over again.

The student template contains only the Hook.

Title
Author(s) Names
Author(s) Contact Information
Hook
- Grab your students' interest.
- Create a hook that students are interested in and want to investigate further.
- Encourage students to ask deeper questions to help guide their inquiry.

SUMMARY

Web inquiry activities can be used in any subject area and grade level. The idea is for students to use data from the Internet to help answer questions. Typical lessons involve already filtered sources from textbooks, videos, or lectures. When we incorporate the Internet, we provide students with opportunities to tie real-world elements into curriculum and content with the potential for inquiry into our classrooms. Web inquiry activities provide a foundation for students to build connections and meaning from the curriculum, and at the same time they engage and interest students. Students need to ask good questions, make predictions, determine relevancy, and present this new information to others.

FURTHER INVESTIGATION

How to Develop Inquiry Oriented Projects. http://www.youthlearn.org/learning/activities/howto.asp.
Inquiry Page. http://inquiry.uiuc.edu/.
Library of Congress: American Memory Project. http://memory.loc.gov.
Web Inquiry Project. http://webinquiry.org/.

REFLECTION

1. How is a Web inquiry activity different from a WebQuest?
2. Why should students only see the Hook in a Web inquiry activity?

3. What is significant about a Web inquiry activity for the student?
4. What is the role of the teacher in a Web inquiry activity?
5. Why is manipulating raw and unfiltered data important for students?

SKILL-BUILDING ACTIVITY

Throughout this chapter, we explored how to create a Web inquiry activity. The focus was on engaging your students with a topical question so that they are motivated to conduct research and discover new information. Through this process, students identify deeper questions and then find raw data on the Internet to help answer those questions. Throughout, students choose appropriate data, manipulate the data, create possible solutions, and present their findings to others.

Your goal now is to create a Web inquiry activity that aligns with your learning standards and is developed around an interesting and doable topical question. You want to identify possible procedures, resources, and tools that your students will need to complete this inquiry activity. This will be a resource for you and other teachers. Remember, your students will see only the Hook. As they proceed through the Web inquiry activity, you will be open to assisting and supporting them in difficult areas.

5

CREATING A
TELECOLLABORATIVE ACTIVITY

A telecollaborative activity is an activity that provides opportunities for students to work with and create information with other students or experts in different locations using online communication tools such as listservs, message boards, real-time chat, and Web-based conferencing. Locations can be as close as down the hall or as far away as around the world.

The benefits of telecollaborative activities are the possibilities to connect through the Internet with other students, teachers, researchers, scientists, politicians, and business leaders around the world. You can connect and communicate if you and they have Internet access.

In this chapter, we will identify and explore telecollaborative activities that you can implement in your classroom, starting with a big idea question and then creating activities that require outside participants to complete. You can create your own telecollaborative activity or you can participate in an activity that has already been created by someone else. Either way, telecollaboration is a terrific learning experience for you and your students.

OVERVIEW

Telecollaboration provides opportunities for students to practice inquiry learning through the process of questioning, reflecting, and manipulating information using the Internet by collaborating and communicating with others. Your students work as a collaborative group to explore and collect information. They then share this new information with classrooms and experts all around the world using telecommunication.

Telecollaborative activities are curriculum based and teacher designed and coordinated. Most have Web sites to share information collected and information about the activity itself. A telecollaborative activity is usually integrated directly into the curriculum and is not an extra activity.

As with any inquiry-oriented activity, your goal as a teacher is to engage your students with good big idea questions and then let your students discover workable answers. The difference between a telecollaborative activity and other inquiry-oriented activities explored throughout this book is the opportunity for students to work with other students and/or experts in the field around the globe on authentic and meaningful problems.

In a telecollaborative activity, your students collect raw data and then share their information with other classes and experts in the field. Once the information is shared, other students and/or experts have the ability to further explore the collection of data to solve problems.

For example, assume you are planning a unit on the Revolutionary War in your social studies class. A typical lesson on this unit may have students read a chapter on the Revolutionary War and then go to the library to find further information on the war so they can write a report for the class.

An enhancement to this activity could include a telecollaborative element by having your students work with another class in a different part of the world. You begin by doing the following:

- Collecting primary source documents on the Revolutionary War from the American Memory Project at http://memory.loc.gov.
- Outlining a debate topic.

- Contacting teachers on ePals at http://www.epals.com to see if there are any interested teachers and classes out there that want to engage in a debate with your students about a topic relating to the Revolutionary War.

A teacher from England responds to your inquiry, agreeing to a classroom debate on a specific big idea question, such as "Can a compromise be reached before war begins?" between the two sides in the Revolutionary War. Imagine the experiences your students will receive debating, via the Internet, during a peace conference with a class from England on Revolutionary War issues and topics. There will be varying perspectives and resources submitted from both classrooms, as well as the awe of the long-distance link. Information gleaned from the classroom debate can be collected on a shared Web site where both classes can add to the information and make changes where necessary. In addition, lessons learned can be documented, and there is also the potential for ongoing dialog with this international classroom.

The above is a good illustrative example of a telecollaborative activity where teachers and students from different geographic locations and cultures have the opportunity to work together on a problem or shared experience. You have two choices: your class can either join a telecollaborative activity, or you as the teacher can create a telecollaborative activity and invite other classes to participate. You will be introduced to both in this chapter.

USING THE INTERNET IN A TELECOLLABORATIVE ACTIVITY

When you are implementing telecollaboration into your classroom, the Internet is the central tool. The Internet helps classes and experts share information and ideas through collaboration and communication using tools such as e-mail, teleconferencing, and chat. It is important to review several ways that information can be shared and then begin assessing what types of tools you currently have available for use and what tools are needed when implementing this type of activity in your classroom.

Types of Tools

When you begin to look at possible telecollaborative activities or when you begin creating a telecollaborative activity of your own, you want to investigate the several ways information can be exchanged using the Internet. Information can be transferred via the Internet through interpersonal activities, appearances, and mentoring. Figure 5.1 provides a graphic of this connection.

Interpersonal activities allow students to actively communicate with other participants using either e-mail on an asynchronous basis (not at the same time) or chat which is used synchronously (at the same time). By using either e-mail or chat, you have many possibilities for interaction through specific settings or environments.

A global classroom is a type of collaborative environment that utilizes a Web site and has all the necessary tools for communication and collaboration to take place. Within this environment, classes can post

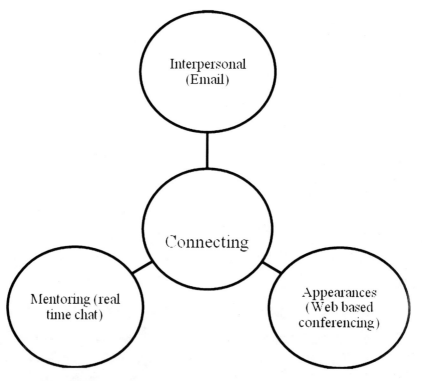

Figure 5.1. Connecting With Others

documents, data, and e-mail or chat with different users. An example of a global classroom is the United Nations Global Classroom found at http://www.globalclassrooms.org/.

Another type of environment is an electronic appearance. These are typically online workshops led and conducted by experts in the field. These appearances typically are led by authors or scientists and allow students to ask questions in order to examine parts of a text or discuss and analyze the new and interesting concepts, such as the latest science invention.

Electronic mentoring is another opportunity for students to ask questions of subject-matter experts from both industry and business. Students have the opportunity to ask questions to help answer specific and necessary questions to help solve a problem. These experts are helping with the telecollaborative activity directly.

Questioning and answering services, such as Ask an Expert (http://www.askanexpert.com/) or the Mad Sci Network (http://www.madsci.org/) provide opportunities for students to ask specific and well-thought-out questions about problems that they have researched and where they need help in finding answers.

In each of these collaborative interactions, the central focus is communication around specific topics as well as working with others, including experts in the field and at a distance. In order to make a telecollaborative activity beneficial for your class, you must prepare for each of these interactions and ensure your students have opportunities for communication and problem solving.

Types of Activities

Once you begin looking at the types and methods of communication, it is now time to identify some possible activities that you and your students can participate in. Always remember to make sure that the activity ties into a specific learning goal. Usually, any learning goal that allows students to practice inquiry skills can be incorporated into this type of activity. Types of inquiry-oriented activities that can easily be integrated into a telecollaborative activity include the following:

- Information collection and analysis activities allow students to collect, compare, contrast, and synthesize complex information that they have collected and evaluated. This information can be posted for other classrooms around the world to access and evaluate. Generally, information collection and analysis involve an online database that can be accessed by all and queried.

- Problem-solving activities provide students with a complex problem that encourages them to critically analyze and synthesize information. This information can be primary or secondary, and they must use this information to present meaningful solutions.
- Types of problem-solving activities may include social action projects, peer feedback activities, and information exchanges. In each of these examples, students examine problems, such as high gas prices, and then use data to determine the best solution for the stakeholders, in this case both the local and global economy.

Whether collecting and analyzing information or problem solving, as the teacher your role is to encourage and guide your students and then provide varied and engaging opportunities for them to research appropriate resources and compile worthwhile information so others can work with the information and help determine possible solutions.

In order for your telecollaborative activity to be successful, there are a few items that you must consider. Remember to do the following:

1. Identify appropriate learning goals and objectives that tie into your standards of learning.
2. Find a partner class or an expert.
3. Develop specific and planned procedures, such that you:
   - Identify how the expert and/or classes will work together.
   - Identify and collect necessary content and resources.
   - Identify specific benchmark dates for data collection, sharing, and presentation.
   - Provide opportunities for reflection and feedback for you and your students throughout the process.

In a telecollaborative activity, students have opportunities to work on similar activities in different locations, cultures, and time zones. This is a major strength of this type of activity, but it also takes planning and specific benchmarks to accomplish the learning goals of the lesson.

To help prepare, you want to ensure that your specific benchmark dates as well as your reflection and feedback opportunities are varied and manageable. This ensures that all students and/or experts at each location can complete their necessary work collecting and sharing information online so that the information is available for all participants to analyze and evaluate.

For example, assume you are a science teacher and you want your students to begin thinking locally as well as globally about the environment and earth systems. You think that this topic could be fully implemented and enhanced if it were offered as a telecollaborative activity. You begin by conducting a search on the Internet and find a possible Internet resource at the GLOBE or "Global Learning and Observations to Benefit the Environment" Web site at http://www.globe.gov.

You read through the GLOBE Web site and find that teachers and students from around the world are conducting primary research and collaborating with scientists from both NASA (National Aeronautics and Space Administration) and NSA (National Science Association). You decide to have your class participate.

As part of the project, it is your responsibility to work with your students to collect quality data in your local area on a specific plant and animal group that is outlined on the GLOBE Web site. Once your class collects the appropriate data, they import the data into the GLOBE database. There are specific benchmarks that must be met so the data can be used by classrooms around the world as well as by NASA and NSA scientists to create a satellite map of specific animal and plant populations around the world.

The data that you and your students collect must be accurate, analyzed and evaluated, and imported into the GLOBE database in a timely manner in order for it to be utilized by actual scientists for their specific deadlines to make predictions on how local data and information impact the global data. As this is a collaborative effort and your students' input impacts the work being done by the scientists at both agencies, it is important to adhere to time requirements; otherwise the results will not be accurate.

This example stresses the need for classes to collect quality data in a timely manner in order for that data to be available for specific groups to use in meaningful ways. In this example, other classrooms and scientists are counting on your students to help fill the database with quality data so real-world predictions and discoveries can be made. This is true real-world collaboration.

THINKING TELECOLLABORATIVELY

The Internet is a powerful tool for schools and classrooms. It provides resources that are timely and abundant, and more importantly it provides access to classrooms and experts around the world on topics that are real and relevant to students and the overall curriculum. A telecollaborative activity combines the benefits of the Internet to provide resources for collaboration and sharing of information.

In order to participate, your classroom needs access to an Internet connection, a meaningful and appropriate project that meets your curriculum needs, and necessary tools to analyze, communicate, synthesize, and share information, such as a spreadsheet, word processing, e-mail, and presentation tools.

In order to incorporate a telecollaborative activity in the classroom, you will need to think differently about the Internet. Typically the Internet is used as a research tool, but it is also a powerful tool to share information through collaboration and communication. One way to use the Internet as a collaboration tool is to create or participate in a telecollaborative activity that ties into your course topics and provides opportunities for your students to think critically about the course topics in new and interesting ways.

One way to begin using the Internet in a standards-based lesson is to provide your students with a relevant problem that is real world and meaningful, and that can be investigated. Once you have a couple of ideas, look for other classrooms and experts that would like to participate.

As mentioned above, when working with others outside the classroom, time is an important consideration. Time must be provided for students to collect data and to provide thoughtful reflection about the data that will ultimately be shared with participating classes. Also, school schedules or schedules of experts must be considered and accounted for when designing or planning to participate in a telecollaborative activity.

When you integrate a telecollaborative activity into your classroom, you are no longer using the Internet solely as a library research tool, but instead you are moving your students toward using the Internet as a critical-thinking and communication tool.

For example, in the telecollaborative activity Underground Railroad (http://exchange.co-nect.net/Teleprojects/project/?pid=), the year is 1850. Students work in collaborative teams and share information with other classes in different locations through a discussion forum. In this activity, students take on the role of a slave during this time period who is attempting to escape from bondage.

The length of time for this telecollaborative activity is 15 days, and the journey requires students to explore, collect, and then share experiences on a group discussion board with classes also taking this journey in different locations around the world.

Planning is important, and time needs to be addressed so that students can explore the content provided in this activity and then share their data and experiences with classrooms also participating in this activity. The research and time spent interacting with other classes to discuss issues, the process, and identifying problems and concerns all need to be considered in terms of deciding time allotments and constraints. Planning is necessary.

HOW TO PLAN FOR A TELECOLLABORATIVE ACTIVITY

Planning involves identifying specific learning objectives and goals. It also includes setting specific benchmarks for your students to collect, analyze, and then share their data with others. In addition, planning time is also spent finding a topic and identifying a specific product that engages your students and increases their understanding of your content area.

In order to do this, you must begin looking at your curriculum. Create a list as shown below to assist you with outlining course topics and themes that you are planning to cover throughout the school year.

Course Topics and Themes
Course topics to be covered with your students this academic year:

1.
2.
3.
4.
5.
6.
7.
8.
9.
10.

From this list, identify three possible themes that are highlighted:

1.
2.
3.

As you identify main topics and key themes that you and your class will be covering for the year, it becomes easier to identify a telecollaborative activity. Planning should always begin by looking at your topics and themes. Next, you need to identify specific standards of learning, as outlined below.

Standards of Learning
Topic(s):
Theme(s):
Learning Standards:

_____

_____

_____

The above topics highlight the learning topics and themes that you identified in your list of topics and incorporate appropriate learning standards.

IDENTIFYING COMPUTER HARDWARE AND SOFTWARE NEEDS

When planning to join a telecollaborative activity already developed by another teacher, you want to first identify what types of computer hardware and software are necessary to participate and make sure your school has the necessary tools. The "Sample Computer Hardware and Software Checklist" provides a check sheet of some possible tools that you may need access to. Make sure when you review and complete this check sheet that you also identify other possible tools that would be helpful for your students to use. Always double check this check sheet when you find a telecollaborative activity to participate in to ensure that you have the necessary tools.

SAMPLE COMPUTER HARDWARE AND SOFTWARE CHECKLIST

Computer Hardware
1. Operating System: Windows, Mac, Linux, Other _____
2. RAM _____ (MB/GB)
3. Hard Drive _____ (MB/GB)
4. Processor (Ghz) _____
5. Internet Connection (circle the correct connection): Dial Up/Modem, Network, Other _____
6. Digital Camera _____
7. Scanner _____
8. Microphone _____
9. Sound Card
10. Digital Video Camera/Web Cam _____
11. Audio Visual Capabilities (Card)

Computer Software
1. Word processing _____
2. Spreadsheet _____
3. Database _____
4. Image Editing _____
5. Presentation _____
6. Video Editing Software _____
7. Web Page Editor _____
8. Draw/Paint _____

Other
1.
2.

VARYING TYPES OF ACTIVITIES

There are many different types of telecollaborative activities with varying ways to share information with others. Therefore, you should be
able to find activities that meet your learning and curriculum needs. It
is important to note that each of the possibilities outlined in the bulleted
list that follows can be combined or completed as stand-alone individual
activities.

The following are two main types of telecollaborative activities (learning opportunities and data collection) that will allow your students to
learn content as well as help you identify specific activities to implement
that will work well with your class.

Learning Opportunities
- Information Exchange

Provides opportunities for your class to share specific and personal
   information of the class or location via e-mail with other classes.
For example, your class may be studying a language or a culture and
   could e-mail a student or class from that particular country or culture.

Data Collection
- Students collect, analyze, and compare different types of information.

Examples include opportunities for students to complete a question-
   naire or to track specific events by collecting primary data.
For example, students collect data on Monarch butterflies to identify
   specific migration paths.
Or students collect local weather data to compile a database on national weather patterns.

In each learning opportunity presented in a telecollaborative activity,
students are able to practice Internet research as well as evaluate information obtained online. Students also have the opportunity to explore
relevant topics and can help find answers to specific questions.

An important element of a telecollaborative activity is that students can explore and review varying answers to and perspectives on the same question and can practice information-seeking and information-evaluating skills. Information seeking is when students investigate and explore topics using research methods. Information evaluating is when students evaluate found information to make sure it is reliable and valid.

When identifying activities that are beneficial to student learning, it is important to choose appropriate learning opportunities around student activities. See the different types of activities below.

- New developed products by those participating in the telecollaborative activity give students an opportunity to create something and share with others.

For example, students could collaborate with other classes around the world to write a specific chapter in a novel about a historical event.

- Primary research opportunities provide students with opportunities to work on complex problems that may not have specific answers.

Students are responsible for developing and comprehending possible hypotheses, identifying necessary resources, collecting data, and then analyzing and manipulating the data by synthesizing the information and then reporting their findings to the collective telecollaborative group.

For example, students could participate and compete in a ThinkQuest project where students in different classrooms around the world create an activity for classrooms to use in their lessons.

- Real-time conferencing with experts and other students in different parts of the world is a way for classrooms to communicate.

Conferencing can be chat or video chat.

Students log on to talk with specific classrooms and experts to share data, synthesize data, and present new and relevant information.

There are many ways that your students can present information to others, such as in written format, letters and stories, data analysis and organization using spreadsheets, graphs and charts, visuals, images and drawings, audio, narration and music, or through multimedia combining these elements plus adding animation. Each of these communication types will allow your students to convey meaning to the information collected and analyzed.

In this planning process, it is important to identify possible ways your students can communicate and exchange their information and files. Students can create a Web site, attach files to e-mail, use file transfer protocol to transfer files from one server to another, input data into an online database, or use conferencing tools that are cross-platform in order to communicate and share files with a wider audience.

Whether you participate in an existing telecollaborative activity or you create an activity yourself, the following guidelines are recommended:

- The activity meets your identified curriculum goals and objectives.
- Your students have opportunities to solve real-world problems that are meaningful to them.
- The topic and themes are integrated seamlessly throughout the activity in order for your students to build knowledge and skills based on your identified standards of learning.
- The activity engages your students to work harder by discovering information and connecting information to prior knowledge.
- Your students have opportunities to communicate with others outside the classroom, such as other students or experts in the field to test their hypotheses.
- Your students have many opportunities to engage in critical-thinking skills, such as comparing and contrasting, analyzing data, researching with primary data, conducting discussions and reflecting on these discussions, and identifying fact from opinion.
- Your students have opportunities to be self-directed in their own learning and as a result begin to develop skills in problem solving.

You want to ensure that the activity allows for active participation for your students along with students in other areas and that the activities are meaningful and allow for hands-on participation from all of your students.

EXISTING TELECOLLABORATIVE ACTIVITY

We explored different activities and ways to communicate and share information, and now it is time to think about participating in an existing telecollaborative activity. It is a good idea to join an existing activity before creating your own activity in order to learn what is necessary to be successful when working with the Internet as a tool for data collection, dissemination, and collaboration with others at different locations around the globe.

When you start researching possible telecollaborative activities, begin by looking at specific directories and e-mail list projects to find a good activity that is appropriate for your class and your content area. In your search, you will find both free and pay-for-service activities that you and your class can participate in. Some examples are:

- iEARN: a nonprofit global network that allows teachers and students to collaborate on real-world issues and concerns using the Internet. http://www.iearn.org/
- Global SchoolNet: links classrooms around the world together with activities and projects that make a difference on a global scale. http://www.globalschoolnet.org/index.cfm
- TEAMS Education Resources: a resource page provided by the Los Angeles County Office of Education. http://teams.lacoe.edu/documentation/projects/projects.html
- IECC: provides opportunities for teachers to connect with other teachers from other cultures and countries through e-mail to utilize pen pals or to set up telecollaborative activities. http://www.iecc.org/
- ePals: another e-mail service for teachers to identify possible telecollaborative activities with classrooms around the world. http://www.epals.com/
- International Telementoring Program: provides mentoring opportunities for classrooms around the world from leaders in business and industry.http://www.telementor.org/

When you first begin a telecollaborative activity, it is best to start small. Look at an activity that involves using e-mail to exchange a message to share information about your community or class, or an activity such as the Global Grocery Project found at http://landmark-project. com/ggl/index.html which allows your students to collect data and add the data to an online database. Either of these simple exchanges will allow you and your students to experience a telecollaborative activity without an extensive time or resource commitment.

For example, the Global Grocery Project allows students to collect local grocery prices to help build a shared database on global food prices that can be used by social studies, science, health, and math classes around the world to analyze and manipulate numerical data to identify varying information. To participate, you would print out a grocery list provided by the project and ask students to identify specific food prices the next time they are at the grocery store. Each student would fill out this grocery price list.

Next time they come to class, the average price for each grocery item on the list is calculated. As a class, you would then submit the average prices into the project's online database. The Global Grocery Project is an easy and fun way to begin a telecollaborative activity. Once you and your students become comfortable collecting and sharing information, you can grow to larger and more involved activities.

By participating in a small activity, your class has an opportunity to share information or add relevant data that are collected over time that can be used by classes all over the world. When you start small, you gain experience and confidence for future telecollaborative activities.

When first starting out, it may be helpful to find another teacher at your school who may additionally want to participate. Another option is to include your technology resource teacher. It is important to have assistance, especially with larger and more involved projects, and to know what resources you will need and have available for use. If you are missing something, can you survive? And if not, you need to determine how you will obtain the necessary resources to be successful.

It is important to identify your technology skill level and determine what assistance you need to complete the activity. Do not be afraid to ask for help. Again, your technology resource teacher is truly an excellent resource in this area and will be happy to participate. Remember also that other classrooms are counting on the data that your students collect and share, so make sure that you are ready and have the necessary support to be successful.

DESIGNING A GOOD TELECOLLABORATIVE ACTIVITY

When you begin the process of designing your own telecollaborative activity, it is a good idea to view some existing projects to give you some ideas. When you begin planning and developing your activity, you want to keep in mind that you are writing for fellow teachers, not your students. In other words, fellow teachers will review the activity guidelines and expectations to determine if they want to participate.

When designing your own telecollaborative activity, there some guiding points that are important to include. You want to identify each of these guiding points in your lesson write-up so other teachers can easily determine if this activity will meet their specific learning goals and needs. The guidelines are as follows:

- Identify learning goals and objectives. Think about what students will be learning and what their activities will be online to learn this new information. Is this an appropriate way for students to achieve these goals?
- Identify appropriate standards of learning. Do they match what you intend for students to learn?
- Ensure that the activity will be easy to implement and continue throughout its duration. Telecollaborative activities involve more than your class. They also involve telecommunications and media tools for both teaching and learning. Is your idea appropriate for these tools and this type of learning?
- Make sure that your students are actively involved throughout the activity and have plenty of opportunity for hands-on experiences. Have you provided quality activities that serve each learning objective's purpose? Are the activities allowing students to critically think about the content?
- Make sure that you collaborate with other schools or experts in the field of study.

- Ensure that you have built in opportunities for continued communication with all participants.
- Ensure that you have built in continuous and appropriate assessments and evaluations of students throughout the activity.
- Ensure that you have clear and doable benchmarks set for all participants to follow.
- Communicate in a timely manner to all participants regarding the closing date of the project and the results of the data obtained once compiled and evaluated.

Once you identify the above guiding points, it is time to begin writing your project goals, topic, theme, and requirements. Make sure that this is clear for all participants to follow. This is also the time to identify how this activity will fit into your curriculum by identifying the appropriate standards of learning.

Within this initial phase of designing your activity, you want to identify who would be good participants, such as earth science classes or English literature classes. Remember, you can encourage cross-curricular participation to incorporate more dynamic data.

Clearly and specifically identify how each participant will communicate and exchange information, such as via e-mail, a discussion forum, a listserv, or Web-based chat. You also want to identify any specific hardware or software requirements. Another important introductory element to include is a clear and doable timeline that includes specific benchmarks for each participant for the duration of the project.

Next, determine how you will compile and distribute the results to the participants once the activity has concluded. And finally, identify both formal and informal methods of evaluation of student work.

It is important to note that you will want to ensure that you have enough participants for your activity to gather good data. Some participants will drop out or not submit all data sets, so you want to make sure that your activity is long enough and has enough people to pull good information from your data.

If your activity has too many participants, this can also be a problem. You want to make sure that you guide some to other groups by suggesting they begin another group, but maintain enough participants to have valuable data.

You are working with other participants, so you want to make sure that you have continued and open contact with them. You want to make sure that you and your class meet all deadlines that you have set, and continually remind participants of deadlines and benchmarks. You also want to continually motivate your students as well as the other participants by letting them know that this is an important activity and the work that they are doing is meaningful and worth the effort.

Be flexible. We all have technology issues, and we may not be aware of our issues when we begin the activity. Make sure that you have support to answer questions when they come up and help with alternative solutions if need be.

The detailed "Sample Telecollaborative Activity" feature shows key areas to focus on and prepare for.

SAMPLE TELECOLLABORATIVE ACTIVITY

Activity Title: Revolutionary War Peace Conference
Project Description:

- Students participating in the Revolutionary War Peace Conference are delegates who will represent opposite points of view on events leading up to the Revolutionary War.
- Students compare and contrast views on the American Revolution from the viewpoint of the monarchy in England as well as the Virginia settlers in the new world.
- Several important issues should be explored by each point of view (above), including:
  - fiscal matters
  - the English monarchy
  - concerns for liberty
  - the Constitution of 1787
  - anti-federalism
- As delegates, students are assigned by the leaders during this time period to help settle their differences. Can it be done?
- Each presentation must highlight the viewpoints of the respective group using video conferencing and ePals.

- Delegates from both points of view will present their arguments back to back, and debate and decide on the spot whether or not a compromise can be reached.
- Delegates will then vote to determine the appropriate wording for the treaty. Hopefully, the Peace Conference is successful!

Instructional Goal(s):
- The overarching goal is for students to know their national heritage as well as the national heritage of others in order to become better-informed participants in shaping the future of the nation.
- During this process of discovery and debate, students begin to understand chronological thinking, connection between causes and effects, and the connection between continuity and change.
- Students also begin the exploration of personal responsibility and why personal responsibility is important, and that ideas, opinions, and experiences have real consequences.
- Through this process of discovery, students understand that events are shaped both by ideas and by the actions of the individual.

Grade Level: Elementary and Middle School

Contact Information of Organizer (name, e-mail, address, phone number, etc.):

Subject Areas: History, Social Science, Geography, Civics, Economics

Learning Standards:
History and Social Science
- Analyze the forces of conflict and cooperation.
- Develop skills in discussion, debate, and persuasive writing with respect to enduring issues and determine how divergent viewpoints have been addressed and reconciled.
- Compare and contrast fundamental political principles, including:
  - constitutionalism and limited government
  - rule of law
  - democracy and republicanism
  - sovereignty
  - consent of the governed
  - separation of powers

- checks and balances
- federalism
- Compare and contrast fundamental liberties, rights, and values, including:
  - religion
  - speech
  - press
  - assembly and petition
  - due process
  - equality under the law
  - individual worth and dignity
  - majority rule
  - minority rights
- Demonstrate skills in historical research and geographical analysis by identifying, analyzing, and interpreting primary and secondary sources and artifacts as well as validating sources as to their authenticity, authority, credibility, and possible bias.

Language Arts
- Identify main ideas and concepts presented in resources.
- Draw inferences, conclusions, or generalizations about text and support them with textual evidence and prior knowledge.
- Distinguish facts, supported inferences, and opinions in text.
- Use organizational features of printed text (e.g., citations, endnotes, and bibliographic references) to locate relevant information.

Number of participants needed for this activity: Two classrooms

Estimated Time: Two weeks, including time to prepare and present

Prior Learning:
Prior to this lesson, students will need to understand the events leading up to the American Revolution and identify recurring themes and/or inconsistencies found in resources.

Directions for Joining the Activity:
This telecollaborative activity will bring together American students with students in England. ePals will be used to gather and share information,

and a video teleconference will be implemented at the end for a peace conference debate.

Hardware and Software Requirements:
Specific software and hardware that will be used for the duration of this activity:

- Telecommunications:
  Required: ePals, Web-based conferencing
  Optional: video conferencing
- Hardware:
  Required: PC, Mac, Linux
  Optional:
- Software:
  Required: e-mail, word processor, concept map
  Optional: video software
- Other:
  Required:
  Optional:

Possible Resources:
Folk Music of England. http://www.contemplator.com/war.html.
Music of the American Revolution. http://members.aol.com/bobbyj164/ mrev.htm.
Spy Letters. http://www.si.umich.edu/spies/.
George Washington Papers. http://lcweb2.loc.gov/ammem/gwhtml/ gwhome.html.http://gwpapers.virginia.edu/.
Queen Charlotte Letters. http://people.virginia.edu/~jlc5f/charlotte/char- lett5.html.
Revolutionary War Timeline. http://www.nps.gov/archive/cowp/ Timeline.htm.
Map Collection. http://memory.loc.gov/ammem/gmdhtml/armhtml/.
Continental Congress. http://memory.loc.gov/ammem/collections/ continental/.
PBS American Revolution. http://www.pbs.org/ktca/liberty/.

Process:
- Task: Students identify major events, themes, and inconsistencies found in resources about the American Revolutionary War.

- Any resource on the Revolutionary War can be used, including textbooks.
- Students need to organize information gathered in order to compare and contrast information and set up an argument to prevent the Revolutionary War.
- On the final day of this activity, students will participate in a debate with the opposing side to convince the leaders not to go into War.

Lesson Preparation
- Search for reliable information on the Revolutionary War.
- Identify recurring themes and possible inconsistencies.
- Small groups will identify specific causes leading to the war.
- Small groups will identify possible solutions to these issues.
- Approximate time: 1 week.

ePals Registration
- Teacher registers project with ePals and locates another teacher or classroom that can participate in this project.
- Students are introduced to the other class through e-mail.

American Revolution Folders
- Teachers prepare ways for students to organize information during the duration of the project, such as using folders, social bookmarking, Web sites, and a database.
- Students collect, analyze, and present information on the events, issues, and causes of the American Revolution.

Day 1
Introduction:
Introduce students to the assignment and procedures/guidelines for this telecollaborative project.

Big Idea Question:
Can you stop the American Revolutionary War?

You will look at what happened. Is there a compromise that could have been reached before the war began? What event or issue could have been prevented from happening?

Meet the Correspondent:
Each class will e-mail the following information about each of the students in the class:

1. Name
2. Age
3. Hometown and country
4. School
5. Hobbies
6. Fun facts
7. Other pertinent information

Events That Brought About the American Revolution:
- Students will e-mail the other class regarding important events that brought about the American Revolution as presented by their history textbooks.
- Students identify political, religious, and economic ideas and interests that brought about the American Revolution, such as the resistance to imperial policy, the Stamp Act, the Townshend Acts, taxes on tea, Coercive Acts, etc.
- Students will create a concept map to share with the other class to identify key issues and their understanding about each.

Day 2
Drafting and Signing of the Declaration of Independence
- Who were the people and the events associated with this document?
- Why was this document important? What did signing this document say to the monarchy in England?
- Share findings through e-mail.
- Identify key points made by both classes.
- Add artifacts and findings into a database for easy retrieval.
- Save resources.

Day 3
- Who were the people making decisions and influencing policy during this time period?
- Share findings through e-mail.

- Identify key points made by both classes.
- Add artifacts and findings into a database for easy retrieval.
- Save resources.

Day 4
- Identify battles, campaigns, and varying turning points within this time period.
- Share findings through e-mail.
- Identify key points made by both classes.
- Add artifacts and findings into a database for easy retrieval.
- Save resources.

Day 5
- What are the specific roles of the British, American, and Indian leaders during this time period?
- Share findings through e-mail.
- Identify key points made by both classes.
- Add artifacts and findings into a database for easy retrieval.
- Save resources.

Day 6
- What were the economic hardships of the everyday person living during this time period? Include families, financing the war, inflation, hoarding goods for profiteering, etc.
- Share findings through e-mail.
- Identify key points made by both classes.
- Add artifacts and findings into a database for easy retrieval.
- Save resources.

Day 7
- Compile data and identify an outline for the debate.
- Share findings through e-mail.
- Both classes will determine key issues to debate and time schedule for each side.
- Share artifacts and resources with other class.
- Save resources.

Days 8 and 9
- Prepare debate around outlined topics and issues.
- Students can use any media to help convey message, such as images, video, animation, text.

Day 10
- Debate via video conference.
- Post Lesson Wrap-up.
- After the debate, students write a final e-mail identifying key take-aways and a final thank you for the effort and work on this collaborative project.

Evaluation of Student Learning:
The evaluation of this project is based on the final research project and whether the students were able to effectively compare and contrast information about the American Revolution.

The following is a rubric that can be used to assess the students' writing of the final research report:

4 (Exceeds Standards)
- Identifies key issues, views, and important events of American Revolution.
- Identifies points of view from different sides.
- Supports views with quality resources.
- Provides a solid argument for viewpoint identifying quality resources, to include primary source documents and historians.
- Well prepared for debate.

3 (At Standard)
- Supports ideas for varying viewpoints.
- Able to identify inferences, conclusions, or generalizations about resources and is able to support with good resources and prior knowledge.
- Able to identify some facts, supported inferences, and opinions in resources.
- Uses varying methods to organize and display information, concept maps, database, images, word processing, etc.

- Supports argument with well-researched ideas surrounding issues and events.

2 (Approaching Standard)
- Able to identify some main ideas and concepts presented in resources.
- Able to draw some inferences, conclusions, or generalizations about resources and support some with textual evidence and prior knowledge.
- Identifies some facts, inferences, and opinions in resources accurately.
- Organizes information well by using some tools to convey meaning of information gathered.
- Supports argument to some extent.

1 (Does Not Meet Standard)
- Identifies few main ideas, concepts, and issues within quality resources.
- Identifies only a few inferences, conclusions, or generalizations about resources and is not able to support them with textual evidence and prior knowledge.
- Identifies a few to no facts, supported inferences, and opinions in text.
- Does not use very many organization methods and does not locate quality information.
- Does not support argument well.

EVALUATING YOUR TELECOLLABORATIVE ACTIVITY

When creating an activity, especially a telecollaborative activity, you want to evaluate its effectiveness to ensure that you are meeting your learning goals and are emphasizing the collaboration and communication tools available as learning tools that engage your students in the process of inquiry learning with classrooms outside your school.

When you look over your activity, make sure that it aligns with the appropriate learning objectives and goals, that it is realistic and doable,

Table 5.1. Sample Telecollaborative Activity Evaluation

Evaluate Your Activity	Yes/No
Learning objectives identified	
Learning goal is clear and accurate	
Standards of learning align with activity	
Are the activities realistic and doable?	
Are the activities clearly aligned with the learning objectives?	
Are the activities appropriately sequenced?	
Can this activity be done better without collaborating with others outside the classroom?	

and that your activities are clearly outlined and appropriately sequenced. Ask yourself: Is this a good activity? Could this be done by reading a Web resource and not working with individuals outside the classroom? An example of an evaluation rubric is provided in table 5.1.

TELECOLLABORATIVE ACTIVITY TEMPLATE

The following is a telecollaborative activity template that you can use in developing your activities.

Activity Title:
Project Description:
Instructional Goal(s):
Contact Information of Organizer (name, e-mail, address, phone number, etc.):
Grade Level:
Subject Areas:
Standards of Learning:
Identify expected prior knowledge of learners:
Who should consider participating?
Number of participants accepted for activity:
Directions for joining the activity:
Specific software and hardware that will be used for duration of activity:
Resources:

Process (specific):
Evaluation of student learning:

SUMMARY

Telecollaborative activities are a great way to utilize the communication and collaboration tools of the Internet. The purpose of a telecollaborative activity is to effectively use the Internet to engage learners by working with other classes or with experts in the field of study using real-world tools.

FURTHER INVESTIGATION

A Virtual Architecture's Web Home. http://virtual-architecture.wm.edu/index.html.

Classroom Projects listserv. http://www.globalschoolnet.org/.

Connect Teleprojects. http://exchange.co-nect.net/Teleprojects/.

ePals. http://www.epals.com/.

Global Grocery Project. http://landmark-project.com/ggl/index.html.

GLOBE (Global Learning and Observations to Benefit the Environment). http://www.globe.gov/.

Harris, J. (2001, May). Teachers as Telecollaborative Project Designers: A Curriculum-Based Approach. *Contemporary Issues in Technology and Teacher Education* 1(3). http://www.citejournal.org/vol1/iss3/seminal/article1.htm.

iEarn. http://www.iearn.org/projects/index.html.

KidLink. http://www.kidlink.org/.

KidProject. http://www.kidlink.org/KIDPROJ/.

Mining the Internet column, The Computing Teacher, Judi Harris. http://lrs.ed.uiuc.edu/Mining/April95-TCT.html.

Telecollaborative Learning Projects. http://www.2learn.ca/Projects/project centre/projintro.html.

REFLECTION

1. How could you integrate a telecollaborative activity into your curriculum?

2. Identify types of learning opportunities and activities that would be beneficial to your students' learning and your own standards of learning for your topic.

3. What are some of the key components to a successful telecollaborative project?

SKILL-BUILDING ACTIVITY

You have explored telecollaborative activities in this chapter; it is now time to begin researching telecollaborative activities that you can participate in with your class. Remember, you will want to start simple and grow in difficulty and involvement. You may want to start using e-mail correspondence. Take a look at the ePals Web site at http://www.epals. com to see if there is a simple activity that will work with your students and class.

After you have participated in a simple activity, it is time to begin the process of finding and participating in a more involved activity. This may be one or two weeks in length and involve your students collecting and sharing data. Remember to find something that is doable and not too overwhelming. Other classes are depending on you, and you want to make sure that you can meet each benchmark.

Lastly, it is time to create your own telecollaborative activity. Identify your learning standards, topics, and resources. Next, determine what activities will help your students meet each of these standards using telecommunication tools. Write your activity down and begin seeking participants. Post on a telecollaborative listserv such as Classroom Projects or post your activity on ePals, KidLink, or KidProject (Web site URLs are provided above in the "Further Investigation" section).

6

ASSESSMENTS AND INQUIRY

As you have discovered throughout this book, inquiry is the act of asking good questions about instructional topics in order to encourage your students to think critically about the world around them. A follow-up to the inquiry process is the application of effective assessments.

When you incorporate inquiry into your classroom, your goal is to create an interactive activity that engages students in the process of thinking, exploring, and asking informed questions. Thinking is an active process that does not end with the activity but rather continues through to your assessments culminating from the activity. You want your inquiry-oriented activities to include assessments that incorporate the same creativity and critical-thinking skills you nurtured and developed throughout your activity.

For purposes of this book, assessment is defined as the process of documenting, in measurable terms, knowledge and skills gained from the lesson or activity. Thus, this means that the big idea questions you identified at the beginning of your lesson and the learning standards that you aligned with your questions should be at the center of your activity.

Each inquiry-oriented activity explored throughout this book focuses on creating engaging and directed experiences through the process of discovery. Students are motivated to ask good questions to learn about the topics that are outlined by you the teacher. In conducting assessments to culminate the activity, why not incorporate these same principles into your assessments by tying them into the activity and ultimately into the big idea question?

You may be wondering how it is possible to tie your big idea question and your assessments together to determine student understanding. This chapter lays out a plan of action for you to do just that and to put your assessments at the center of your inquiry-oriented activity.

OVERVIEW

In the classroom, assessments provide an opportunity for learning and feedback for both you and your students. If you keep this line of thought when you develop your assessments, it becomes easier for you to creatively integrate assessments throughout your unit, especially when implementing inquiry-oriented activities.

As teachers, we typically do not think of assessments as learning tools but instead as dreaded events that happen at the end of a learning unit. If you change this idea of assessments and incorporate assessments throughout the unit, you provide not only a refreshing way to evaluate student progress but also a good tool for both you and your students to gauge their understanding of the material.

In identifying your learning standards, you thought about, developed, and then asked your students big idea questions to help guide their interests and to ensure they stayed focused on the important concepts to be explored and discovered.

Once you identify your learning standards and the big idea questions, you begin to identify ways in which your students can best demonstrate understanding. From here, you move toward identifying strategies for integrating continuous assessments throughout your unit. The effective use of continued assessments ensures that students are on task and are gaining the necessary knowledge based on your learning objectives that you outlined at the beginning of your unit.

To do this, you need to plan your assessments right from the very beginning of your unit. The idea of planning assessments at the beginning of a unit may sound foreign but think about it. If assessments are viewed as a learning tool, why not incorporate them throughout your unit and begin thinking about assessments at the very beginning in your design stage?

For example, suppose that your next unit is on mathematical fractions. You decide that you want to incorporate a telecollaborative activity into your lesson on fractions to help students discuss important concepts and rules related to fractions as well as to help them identify important real-world uses of fractions.

You identify an important standard of learning that aligns with the unit on fractions:

- Students will demonstrate knowledge of how to name and write fractions represented by drawings and concrete materials. This activity will also help students understand the difference between the numerator and denominator of a fraction and how to determine each.

Guiding questions could include:

- How can I express fractions verbally, visually, and in writing?
- What questions are important for me to ask about fractions and their relationship to other mathematical concepts I have learned about?
- How do fractions play a role in my everyday world?

Next, you need to determine what key understandings your students will gather from this unit. Some possibilities are:

- Key terms such as divisor and numerator.
- Strategies for solving fraction problems such as adding, subtracting, and multiplying fractions.
- Analyzing the results for specific problems numerically and visually.
- General uses of fractions in daily life to help solve real-world problems.

Once you determine what is important for your students to understand, it is time to choose appropriate assessments in order to determine if in fact they understand. Some possibilities to check student understanding might include:

- Quiz on relevant terms.
- Work on problems related to real-world examples.
- Ask questions about specific problems they encounter in the real world and have students explain and draw their thinking process of solving each.
- Work in small groups to build a birdhouse using fractions.
- Have students self-assess by creating blueprints for their birdhouse design.
- Observe students' processes and procedures to determine if students understand.
- Ask higher-order thinking questions to help students discover new information and to pinpoint possible problems in students' thinking.
- Use "Ask an Expert" to ask questions of math experts and then in large groups reflect on answers.
- Create a Web site to share new understandings of fractions with other students in future classes and in other schools.

Next, you can look at what telecollaborative opportunities are in existence that your students can participate in. Possibilities include:

- Math TV Problem Solving Videos: A telecollaborative project where students learn about mathematical concepts through video creation (available at http://www.mathtv.org/).
- The National Math Trail: A telecollaborative project that ties together specific math problems with opportunities to share possible solutions (available at http://www.nationalmathtrail.org/).
- Mathematics Virtual Learning Circle: A project that provides opportunities for students to explore math as it relates to the real world (available at https://media.iearn.org/node/143).

- Connecting Math to Our Lives: A telecollaborative project that ties math into family life (available at http://media.iearn.org/projects/math).

The idea is to use your big idea questions to help guide your students through the process of learning (in this case mathematical fractions) as they discover firsthand knowledge about how these broad but interesting concepts relate to their world and at the same time guide your students through the process of learning by incorporating meaningful assessments.

As you can see, this chapter helps guide you through structuring your inquiry activity with continuous assessments in order to determine if your students understand the intended learning goals and are achieving the desired results.

FOCUS ON LEARNING AND UNDERSTANDING

Inquiry learning and the different activities that we have explored in this book provide opportunities for student learning through engagement. Part of this engagement comes through continued assessment. Assessments aid teachers *and* students by helping them determine if the desired results of the lesson are being achieved.

As a teacher, you use many different assessment strategies throughout a lesson to determine if your students are gaining the necessary information and to ensure that they can move forward with the lesson. Inquiry-oriented activities are no different.

Assessments take many forms, informally through observations, questioning techniques, small and large group work, think-pair-share strategies, and more formally through quizzes and project performances. Other types of assessments include student self-assessments such as portfolios and learning logs. The key to any effective assessment strategy is to incorporate assessments throughout your unit to ensure student understanding and not only at the end of a unit through a summative evaluation.

Continued assessment provides opportunities for you as the teacher to determine both a student's performance and his or her specific understandings of the topics being explored. This provides you with opportunities to guide students and provide feedback to help them get on track if needed or to surge ahead with the activity.

As we learned in chapter 1, Bloom's taxonomy provides a guide to create activities that encourage students to apply new knowledge and to synthesize this new knowledge by analyzing and asking important questions. To do this successfully, students must understand the broad topics, not just specific tasks and skills. Students then need to be able to apply these broad understandings in meaningful performances.

An example of a meaningful performance as it relates to an inquiry-oriented activity could be having students identify issues and conflicts within the U.S. Civil War. Students could complete a think-pair-share activity to get the discussion started. First, you could ask students to think about and write down everything they know about the Civil War, including any major events that came before the war.

Students then can be paired in small heterogeneous groups to discuss and share what they wrote down. As a group, they can choose three issues and/or conflicts that they want to share with the class. A member of the group can walk up to the interactive white board to write the group's three issues and/or conflicts on the board. As a class, the issues and conflicts could be grouped, discussed, and saved for later discussion.

This is a form of assessment. This assessment allows the teacher to identify and direct student understanding about the issues and conflicts of the American Civil War. As students identify the main issues of this war, the teacher can ask guiding questions to get students to identify misperceptions or to bring in other issues that are being missed by the students to emphasize specific points.

Assessments provide opportunities for students to tie in prior understanding and personal connections about the topics explored as well as help both students and teachers to determine what is understood and what needs further clarification about the topics within the activity.

As the activity continues and students begin tying their interests into what they are learning, you want to provide opportunities for students to build on their knowledge and to continuously demonstrate their understanding. With each step, you want to guide your students through the process of inquiry using questions and instructional problems as a learning tool. These learning tools are also forms of assessment.

As students build their personal connections around the major goals of the activity, you want your assessments to continue as well. Build on questions, tie in research, and have students continuously share information with their classmates and with you. Entice students to debate with their classmates and possibly with students from outside the class. Throughout this process, you are facilitating the experience in order to ensure that your students are on task, are engaged, and understand what is important.

As students dig deeper and get more involved with the content, they also begin to have a richer experience in terms of more deeply exploring the lesson and discovering new information. Throughout this process, the student and teacher identify benchmarks or performance tasks to ensure that the student is on task. As the teacher, you continually evaluate your students by having them share their findings with others and outline specifically what they learned by discussing and presenting their findings.

The idea of continued assessments is not to wait until the end of an activity to provide feedback to the student through a summative assessment, but instead to provide measures of performance that involve dynamic and diverse opportunities for reflection and feedback throughout the activity. This helps provide guidance and ensures direction.

IDENTIFYING BENCHMARKS

It is important for you to identify concrete benchmarks from your learning standards and goals. A benchmark is what you want your students to understand at specific points in an activity.

For example, let's say that you identify a math standard that asks students to explore and manipulate mathematical models in your math class. You want to provide a real-world learning experience, so you have students look at seasonal temperatures along a specific latitude and longitude of the atlas.

You find that a Web inquiry activity will work perfectly for this activity and standard. You provide students with an online database, such as http://worldclimate.com. At this Web site, up-to-date information and data are stored on temperatures around the world. Students use this weather database to collect raw data and then in collaborative groups they place the data in a spreadsheet.

Once students place the data in the spreadsheet, the class can convene in a large group to discuss equations to help pull out the necessary data to answer the big idea questions. As the teacher, you test student understanding of the data collected and the mathematical models needed to solve the necessary problems, such as to predict temperatures in different geographical regions.

The benchmarks for this example could be placed in several different locations of this activity. One is a brainstorming activity where you ask students about the world map. Next, you can identify and discuss the difference between longitude and latitude and have students hypothesize what the differences mean to weather.

You could introduce climates in various topographies and structures and then question students to interpret and analyze information gathered from the database at the Web site. This allows them to identify the differences and importance of relative and absolute locations and values such as elevation. Another benchmark could be located after students collect the necessary data from the online database.

In small groups, students could outline different mathematical models that could be used to answer questions about the activity. One question could be "What does the height of the sun have to do with Earth's surface temperature?"

In order for students to get started with this assignment, you need to determine what basic information they need to begin their quest. This involves vocabulary and definition of key terms such as data, average temperature, correlation, regression, and trend lines.

Continuing and expanding this activity, students can be further engaged in discovering relationships between location and physical and climatic regions along a specific longitude and latitude, and then they can consider problems such as population and density, industry, vegetation, and climate. You could also introduce additional Web sites, such as http://CIAworldfactbook.gov, for students to collect data on items such as population, cities, and topography.

In each of the activities described above, students are actively involved by asking questions and exploring possible answers. You identify where students should be at each point of the activity and ascertain the answer to the important question, which is: What should my students know at this point and how can I identify when or if they know it? These benchmarks are also shared with your students so they also understand what is important. Table 6.1 outlines possible benchmarks for this sample activity.

IDENTIFYING YOUR ESSENTIAL QUESTIONS

When you look at your big idea inquiry activity, you want to ask yourself some questions to help guide you through the design of your unit and to identify what is important for your students to understand from the unit itself.

First, to add a real-world element to your unit, ask yourself why it is so important to study this unit, anyway. You know your students are thinking this very question, so it is helpful if you can provide a real-world rationale for why this unit is important to them. For example, it is important to understand the basics of mathematical models so that the impact of temperature and ultimately global climates can be determined.

Next, you want to ask yourself what makes this unit universal in scope, meaning how it applies to other units and other subject areas. All instructional pieces combine and mix, so ask yourself how your topic combines and mixes with other topics and subjects. For example, what is the connection between mathematical models as they relate to temperature and the topical areas of geography, history, social studies, English, science, and math?

Table 6.1. Identifying Benchmarks

Explore and manipulate a mathematical model that highlights temperature and climate.	• Discuss key terms and definitions. • Discuss topography and climate differences. • Identify necessary data from database. • Identify correct mathematical models.

In addition, topics discussed tend to have an underlying issue or problem, so it is important to determine what this is. Identifying the underlying problem helps to grab the interest of your students and it also allows you the opportunity to identify benchmarks and assessment opportunities. One core question you can ask yourself is what would hinder your students if they just did not get it.

As noted earlier, we also want to tie our topics into the bigger picture and relevant, real-world events. How does your topic tie into your students' world? You want to be specific here by spelling it out. This ties into why it is important for students to study this particular topic. If they did not, they would be missing a large part of their world. Figure 6.1 identifies three major questions to help identify essential questions.

IDENTIFYING LEARNING ACTIVITIES

When you look at assessments in your planning stage, you want to focus on what your intended outcomes are. For example, if your standards

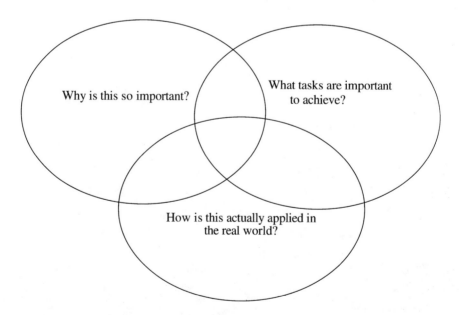

Figure 6.1.   Identifying Essential Questions

state that students must be aware of appropriate nutrition requirements for their weight and age group, then you want them to understand the USDA food pyramid guidelines.

Benchmarks that you can set for this activity would be to have students plan daily diet intakes for different age groups and in different settings. Students could analyze their own eating habits as well as those of family members. A big idea question to consider would be "Why do people eat the way they do?"

A specific task that you can ask students to complete to determine if they understand this big idea is to have students plan a menu for diverse groups as well as survey people asking them why they eat what they do. You could also have students complete a quiz on the USDA food pyramid to ensure that they understand the basic concepts of food and its relationship to one's health. Finally, you could also ask them to reflect on their families' eating habits compared to other groups that they have studied thus far in the lesson.

In planning your unit, you want to determine what types of evidence you need to determine if students understand the important concepts of your lesson. For example, you can incorporate exercises to increase opportunities of your students' discovery of specific points and then have them compare and contrast their findings.

Next, ask yourself what specific responses you are looking for to determine if students understand. What determines a correct response or an incorrect response? This is where you create a rubric and criteria to determine student learning. Finally, you want to determine if the evidence that you identified as important actually aligns with your goals and objectives for your unit. Are students learning what you intended?

Questions for you to consider are:

- What learning activities will strengthen my students' understanding?
- What performances will highlight student work and align with my learning goals?
- What types of evidence will my students need to complete to determine their understanding and strengthen their learning?
- What criteria should I highlight to determine quality of student work?

• What types of assessments can I utilize to determine who really understood compared to those that only partially understood?

In inquiry-oriented learning, you want your students to actively participate and think about the concepts in the activity like a professional would. For example, what would a historian ask about the American Civil War? What would a scientist ask about mathematical models? Students should have the opportunity to use primary source documents to compare and contrast and to think critically about topics that impact their world. Allowing them to conduct primary research enables them to formulate important questions to help find solutions.

Small teams provide students with opportunities to discuss and debate issues around topics. Throughout the entire inquiry activity, you can assess your students through observation, feedback, and performances. You want them to rehearse and practice tasks, give and receive feedback, and perform by creating meaningful products.

IDENTIFYING CRITERIA

Identifying criteria for what students are to accomplish during an inquiry-oriented activity is an important element to student learning. Rubrics are a good example of teachers identifying key learning criteria for students in an activity. Rubrics provide a concise measurement tool to identify what is important for students to accomplish and ultimately to understand about the activity itself.

When you provide a rubric in the beginning of an activity, you allow students to see what you think is important about the activity, and they can work toward each identified criterion in the rubric throughout the activity itself.

Rubrics are a form of benchmark. They are indicators of understanding. Rubrics provide your students with a score in order for them to determine where they are in the process. The more intense and specific your rubric is, the more students know what your expectations are.

It is important to remember that rubrics are only as good as you design them. The more specific your expectations are and the more your rubric is aligned with your learning standards, the better your rubric.

For example, if you were to create a rubric for your lesson on mathematical models, you would have several expectations and criteria to determine what students understood as well as how they performed on each specific task. Table 6.2 provides an example of a rubric that could be developed for the mathematical model activity.

SUMMARY

Throughout your inquiry-oriented activity, you created a very robust learning experience for your students. You tied experiences into your learning standards, and you incorporated real-world elements that would ignite your students' interest and motivation into the process of thinking and ultimately learning.

As you identified your learning standards, you also outlined your objectives. Next, you outlined specifically how your students could demonstrate their understanding throughout this activity. You did this by identifying important benchmarks or places within the lesson that provided you and your students with knowledge on how they were doing at that point in the activity. Are they understanding? Do they need some guidance to help them move forward?

As benchmarks were identified, you also began thinking about what tasks you wanted your students to complete in order to demonstrate understanding. What performances do you want them to complete to ensure that they understand? Throughout the activity, you want to ensure that both informal and formal assessments are embedded.

Informal assessments provide opportunities for both you and your students to ask questions to determine if they are on target with what is important in the lesson to understand. Informal assessments can include questions as well as observations. Peer feedback and evaluations can also be a form of informal assessment. Informal assessments are not intended to be used for a grade but instead as a measuring tool that determines where students are in their understanding of the material.

Formal assessments, in contrast, include quizzes, tests, projects, and activities. As the teacher, you provide feedback on these assessments and allow students to ask questions and develop their understanding.

Table 6.2. Rubric for Mathematical Models Lesson

Category	Advanced	Proficient	Basic	Below Basic
Students are able to describe and represent mathematical relations using tables.	Data in the table are well organized, accurate, and easy to read.	Data in the table are organized, accurate, and easy to read.	Data in the table are accurate and easy to read.	Data in the table are not accurate and/or cannot be read.
Students are able to describe and represent mathematical relationships using graphs.	The graph is exceptionally well designed, neat, and attractive. A ruler and graph paper (or graphing computer program) was used.	The graph is neat and relatively attractive. A ruler and graph paper (or graphing computer program) was used.	Line is neatly drawn but the graph appears quite plain.	The graph appears messy and "thrown together" in a hurry. Line is visibly crooked.
Units on graph.	All units are described (in a key or with labels) and are appropriately sized for the data set.	Most units are described (in a key or with labels) and are appropriately sized for the data set.	All units are not described (in a key or with labels) or are not appropriately sized for the data set.	Units are neither described nor appropriately sized for the data set.
Students are able to create rules to explain the relationship between numbers when a change in the first variable affects the second variable.	Rules accurately represent the data and are written in standard form.	Rules accurately represent the data but are not written in standard form.	Rules represent some of the data.	Rules do not represent the data.
Calculation of normal temperature around the globe using a mathematical model.	Uses rules to correctly calculate normal temperature around the globe in degrees Celsius to the nearest tenth.	Uses rules to correctly calculate normal temperature around the globe in degrees Celsius to the nearest degree.	Calculates normal temperature around the globe in degrees Celsius to within 5 degrees.	Does not calculate normal temperature around the globe in degrees Celsius or calculates with an error over 5 degrees.

You provide guidance and structure to ensure that students are grasping what is important from the activity.

It is important in each activity that you provide enough support for your students to learn and grow in their understanding of the topics explored. In order to do this, continuous rather than summative assessments are needed. Remember that the goal of inquiry-based learning is to ensure that students understand. You do this by tying in real-world experiences and problems, which ultimately increases engagement and understanding of the activity.

In each of the activities explored in this book, there have been many opportunities to assess student understanding. In this task, you want to ensure that you are not waiting until the end to evaluate your students but that you identify your criteria early, share these criteria with your students, and then ensure that they are on task and are understanding throughout the activity itself.

FURTHER INVESTIGATION

Rubistar. http://rubistar.4teachers.org/.
Rubrics for Teachers. http://www.rubrics4teachers.com/.
Using Rubrics in Middle School. http://www.middleweb.com/rubricsHG.html.
Why use Rubrics? http://www.teach-nology.com/tutorials/teaching/rubrics/.

REFLECTION

1. Why is continuous assessment important in an inquiry-oriented activity to enhance student learning?
2. Identify three different assessments that you could use to determine if students understand an important topic within an inquiry-oriented activity?
3. Why are benchmarks important when planning for assessments within an inquiry-oriented activity?
4. How do rubrics improve student learning in an inquiry-oriented activity?

SKILL-BUILDING ACTIVITY

It is time to incorporate continuous assessments throughout your inquiry-oriented activity. Revisit an inquiry-oriented activity and review your learning standards, topics, and resources. Write down four specific benchmarks you want your students to achieve. Next, determine what activities will help your students meet each of these benchmarks. Write down each activity, highlighting the standards of learning (SOLs) for each one. Design and develop a rubric that aligns with your identified SOLs and identify specific criteria. Ask a colleague to review your benchmarks, rubric, and standards. What is their opinion? Are your learning assessments meaningful? Do they align with your standards? Is your rubric helpful and accurate?

7

INQUIRY IN EDUCATION USING TECHNOLOGY

Throughout the activities explored in this text, inquiry has been continually emphasized and stressed. Technology is used as a tool to engage students in the process of learning as well as to provide a real-world element to the lesson.

In a lesson that integrates technology, the technology itself does not take the lead role but rather is used to communicate, analyze, and present information. This chapter further explores and expands upon the integration of technology as a tool to further engage your students in inquiry.

OVERVIEW

Technology tools and the Internet have the potential to enhance lessons in a classroom, but when the tools also encourage inquiry, then student engagement can increase even more. For example, visit the Peace Corps "World Wise Schools" Web site at http://www.peacecorps.gov/wws. This Web site was created for teachers to integrate cross-cultural lessons, stories, activities, and videos into their classrooms to engage students in conversation about different cultures and service learning.

Within the Web site, students are able to read letters, see videos, and listen to podcasts from Peace Corp volunteers about their field experiences. When you incorporate these technology tools into your classroom instruction and allow your students instant access to these real-world expeditions, your students become more engaged and are able to ask meaningful questions about culture, language, and global society. It is important to continually ask yourself how these technology tools and activities focused on engagement tie into your learning standards to ensure that your students are learning what is expected.

This chapter highlights how technology can be integrated into your inquiry unit to engage students to ask essential questions in order to dig deeper into the big issues that surround us as a global society. Questions regarding war and peace, gender and race equality, global warming, homelessness, health care, and education equity are major societal issues that can be set forth to students at different levels so that they can formulate the questions. You can then help them explore the results using technology tools and an integrated technology lesson plan while at the same time tying in your standards of learning revolving around your course topics of math, science, history, language, and the arts.

TECHNOLOGY MUST SUPPORT CURRICULAR GOALS

Any technology tool that is used in the classroom to engage students in inquiry must emphasize curriculum goals. Technology tools are best utilized in a classroom when they enhance active engagement of the learner, utilize collaborative groups, encourage feedback and interaction, and provide connection to experts in the field of study.

In this twenty-first century, technology touches many aspects of our everyday lives. We can communicate via the Internet, receive data from satellites, and record progress through digital images. Technology in the classroom has the potential to provide students with experiences that they will encounter in the world of work or in their everyday lives. Having students interact with technology provides meaning, relevancy, and application in the lesson.

Technology integration means more than teaching students how to use a word processor. Integrating technology successfully into a lesson means using the Internet, digital cameras, and software applications as tools that engage your students in meaningful work.

Inquiry-oriented activities can help provide students with meaningful classroom lessons and activities by having them work with diverse, relevant, and interesting data as well as provide students with opportunities to express themselves through images, sound, and text.

Technology tools are best integrated when they are student driven: for example, when the students gather relevant and timely data, then aid in analyzing and synthesizing that data, and later present the data in meaningful ways to the rest of the class. In an inquiry-oriented activity, technology tools can help teachers offer students the ability to do the following:

- Access relevant data in a timely manner such as through the use of primary source documents.
- Collect and record information, such as through the use of an Internet database or spreadsheet.
- Collaborate with experts and other students around the world, such as by asking an expert and ePals (http://www.epals.com/).
- Present information through multimedia, such as with the use of images, sound, and/or text.
- Have meaningful and authentic assessments, such as real-world problems and projects.
- Present new student knowledge to the world for review and feedback.

MEANINGFUL LEARNING

When adjusting your lessons to an inquiry approach to teaching and learning, try to move away from using technology solely to deliver content. Instead, seamless technology integration becomes the link to creating engaging inquiry-oriented activities that would be impossible to achieve without integrating technology tools. Table 7.1 provides an outline of moving up Bloom's taxonomy using technology integration as a tool.

Table 7.1. Bloom's Taxonomy and Technology Integration

Bloom's Taxonomy:	Remember	Understand	Apply	Analyze
Engage	• Recognize • List • Describe • Name • Locate	• Interpret • Summarize • Infer • Paraphrase • Compare • Explain	• Implement • Use information • Execute tasks	• Compare • Organize • Structure • Integrate
Collaborate	• Presentation given by the teacher on a topic. • Bookmarking a Web page for future use.	• Journal using a blog with a focus on simply writing a task-specific entry.	• Students choose a software program or operate and manipulate hardware and software applications. • Students apply new knowledge to tasks.	• Students create mashups where several data sources are combined into a single set of usable information to create meaning, such as in GoogleLitTrips.
Constructivist	• Use a social bookmarking tool, such as Delicious, to store Web sites for the class to access from any computer with an Internet connection.	• Use a microblog, such as Twitter, to write brief entries sharing information with group members.	• Share and manipulate content on shared networks, such as Flickr or Wikis.	• Students connect information through links within documents and Web pages in order to clarify, analyze, and synthesize content.

Authentic	• Conduct a key word search using only key words or terms.	• Categorize, comment, and annotate Web pages.	• Add, remove, and alter content on Web sites in order to add to the body of knowledge, such as Wikipedia.	• Compare and contrast information. • Question information and lead discussions on the information from experts in the field. • Reflect on learning through careful blogging and participate on experts' blogs.
Standards	• Teachers set learning goals. • Teachers use technology as delivery devices. • Teachers use the tool in a basic way.	• Activities are monitored by the teacher. • Results are evaluated with some reflection from students. • Some integration of technology goes beyond simple drill and practice.	• More student-centered activities. • Incorporate more metacognition from the student that would not be available without technology tools.	• Students take more control of their own learning. • Students become active participants by identifying their prior knowledge and new understandings. • Students ask deeper questions of content and determine what is important to understand.

INSTRUCTIONAL TECHNOLOGY TOOLS

Technology tools can be accessed directly from your computer, such as a Web browser or a word processing program. Or they can be accessed and manipulated directly on the Internet, such as an image editing program or video editing program. Determine what types of tools you have available and which tools will best allow your students to explore the big idea questions you identified for them in order to gain the essential understanding of your content.

One simple way to select appropriate technology for each of your learning tasks is to consider the following:

- What types of learners are your students? Are they visual, verbal, musical, kinesthetic, interpersonal, intrapersonal, logical, naturalist, existential?
- What are your learning objectives?
- From past lessons, what did your students not understand?
- Which technology tool(s) do you have available to you?

For example, let's assume that you want your students to understand that literature mirrors life, language, and culture. In the past, you had students read a literary work, discuss major themes, and then write a paper on these major themes. At the end of the unit, you found that your students were unable to connect the themes and could not relate the themes to real-life events or ideas.

To address these issues, you research the possibility of creating an inquiry-oriented activity and integrating technology into your lesson. Your goal is to engage your students into the major themes of the literary works you are going to read throughout the semester. You also want them to share their understanding with others in a global context. See table 7.2 for an example.

As you conduct your research, you discover GoogleLitTrips (available at http://googlelittrips.com), a virtual world that allows students to study and explore literature through the creation of maps that incorporate multimedia elements. This map with the inclusion of the multimedia elements is called a mashup and it allows your students to add place

Table 7.2.   Identifying Technology Tools

Student Needs
- Visual
- Verbal
- Musical
- Kinesthetic
- Interpersonal
- Intrapersonal
- Logical
- Naturalist
- Existential

Learning Objectives
- Study two characters in the reading.
- Evaluate each character and compare these figures' accomplishments and setbacks.
- Design an appropriate presentation that includes video, sound, and text to tell the characters' story.

What did students not understand from past lessons?
- How to analyze and synthesize information from literary works.
- How to relate the literary works to major themes and issues of the author's era as well as society at large.

Technology Tools Utilized
- Students read and then discuss literary themes in a class discussion and then share their thoughts and analysis about the discussion on a classroom blog.
- Students work in small groups to research specific characters and places within the story.
- The research consists of gathering primary source data, such as images, sound files, video, and Web resources, to highlight student understanding of the characters.
- Students then have opportunities to create artifacts such as video, sound files, Internet resources, and text and to incorporate these into their presentation.
- Students combine the multimedia elements and place on GoogleEarth in order to share with the GoogleLitTrips global audience.

marks on GoogleEarth that can contain video, sound, images, hyperlinks, and/or text.

TWENTY-FIRST-CENTURY SKILLS

As you think about your inquiry-oriented activity and how best to integrate technology tools, it is important to include twenty-first-century skills, such as communication, managing projects, and using technology, as well as the National Educational Technology Standards (NETS) developed by the International Society for Technology in Education (ISTE).

By incorporating inquiry-oriented learning into your lessons, you move beyond basic subject or content mastery to more sophisticated thinking about real-world skills and ideas. As discussed earlier in this book, inquiry-oriented activities allow your students to use higher-order thinking skills, such as analysis, evaluating, and creating (see table 7.3). It also follows, then, that it is important to utilize rubrics as an assessment tool to guide your students and focus them on what is important to understand about the inquiry-oriented activity.

The National Educational Technology Standards also provide standards of integrating technology tools into teaching and learning to enhance the following student skills:

- Creativity and innovation, such as developing innovative products and processes.
- Communication and collaboration, such as using technology tools to support learning.
- Research and information fluency, such as using technology tools to gather, evaluate, and utilize information.
- Critical thinking, problem solving, and decision making, as well as the ability to analyze and synthesize new knowledge.

Table 7.3. Higher-Order Thinking

Higher-Order Thinking and Bloom's Taxonomy	
Analyze	• Explain
	• Classify
	• Investigate
	• Illustrate
Evaluate	• Justify
	• Debate
	• Recommend
	• Decide
Create	• Combine
	• Invent
	• Design
	• Compose

- Digital citizenship, such as an understanding of ethical uses of technology and equity issues.
- Technology operations and concepts, to include understanding the language, systems, and operations of technology tools.

As you design your inquiry-oriented activity, you additionally identify how you want your students to demonstrate their understanding of the major concepts and themes they are exploring. Ask yourself the following questions:

- Can technology provide a medium for my students to best express themselves and share their new knowledge with others in a meaningful way?
- What will students be able to do or know once they finish this inquiry activity and how can they best share this with others?
- How can real-world examples or artifacts be integrated into this inquiry-oriented activity to engage students and to get them to think and explore the bigger picture?
- How can technology enhance these examples, such as by incorporating ideas or discussions of experts into our classroom by using a resource such as ePals or a Weblog?

SUMMARY

The critical takeaway from this chapter discussion is the importance of using technology tools that will help your students achieve their learning goals. The implementation of real-world, authentic, inquiry-oriented activities into your classroom means integrating technology tools seamlessly in ways that are meaningful and provide real-world application. When designing inquiry-oriented activities, your goal is to create instructional tasks that have students finding, evaluating, and synthesizing information from a variety of sources. Some source examples are the American Memory Project at the Library of Congress found at http://memory.loc.gov/ to gather primary source artifacts or a database at the U.S. Fish and Wildlife Organization located at http://www.fws.gov/refuges/databases/tes.html to collect data on endangered species by habitat. The possibilities are endless.

FURTHER INVESTIGATION

Framework for 21st Century Learning. http://www.21stcenturyskills.org.
International Society for Technology in Education (ISTE). http://www.iste.
  org.
National Educational Technology Standards (NETS). http://www.iste.org/AM/
  Template.cfm?Section=NETS.
Technology Integration Matrix. http://fcit.usf.edu/matrix/index.html.

REFLECTION

1. Identify learning objectives that emphasize Bloom's taxonomy.
2. How does your inquiry activity emphasize twenty-first-century skills?
3. Determine how you can integrate technology into your inquiry-oriented lesson to highlight collaboration and communication skills.

SKILL-BUILDING ACTIVITY

Throughout this chapter, the discussion explored in depth how inquiry and inquiry activities can be integrated with technology in order to provide meaningful, real-world experiences to students. The general idea of an inquiry-oriented activity is to engage students through big idea questions and to provide them with learning activities that engage them in discovery and investigation. In order for students to be properly engaged, you want to highlight the higher-order thinking skills of analysis, evaluation, and creativity. Your goal now is to find ways to effectively integrate technology tools with your learning objectives and emphasize real-world skills.

APPENDIX: RESOURCES

CHAPTER 1: WHAT IS INQUIRY?

Bloom, B. S. (1956). *Taxonomy of Educational Objectives, Handbook I: The Cognitive Domain*. New York: David McKay.

Bransford, J., Brown, A., & Cocking, R. Eds. (1999). *How People Learn*. National Research Council. Washington, D.C.: National Academy Press. http://www.nap.edu/openbook/0309065577/html/index.html.

Connect to the Classroom: Inquiry-Based Learning. http://www.thirteen.org/edonline/concept2class/inquiry/index.html.

Exploratorium: The Museum of Science, Art and Human Perception at the Palace of Fine Arts. http://www.exploratorium.edu/.

Integration: Building 21st-Century Learning Environments. http://www.landmark-project.com/edtechnot_warlick/.

Krathwohl, D. R., Bloom, B. S., & Masia, B. B. (1973). *Taxonomy of Educational Objectives: The Classification of Educational Goals, Handbook II: The Affective Domain*. New York: David McKay.

Learning for the 21st Century. http://21stcenturyskills.org/downloads/P21_Report.pdf.

YouthLearn: An Introduction to Inquiry-Based Learning. http://www.youthlearn.org/learning/approach/inquiry.asp.

CHAPTER 2: SETTING UP AN ACTIVITY: TYING GOOD QUESTIONS TO OBJECTIVES

Big Ideas. http://www.authenticeducation.org/bigideas/.

Bloom, B. S. (1984). *Taxonomy of Educational Objectives*. Boston: Allyn & Bacon.

From Now On: The Question Is the Answer. http://fno.org/oct97/question .html.

From Now On: Promoting Thinking and the Growth of Thinkers. http://fnopress.com/pedagogy/modules/toc.htm.

Goetz, E., Alexander, P., & Ash, M. (1992). Understanding and Enhancing Students' Cognitive Processes. In *Educational Psychology: A Classroom Perspective*. New York: Merrill.

CHAPTER 3: CREATING A WEBQUEST

Best WebQuests. http://www.bestWebQuests.com/.

Dodge, B.: A Rubric for Evaluating WebQuests. http://WebQuest.sdsu .edu/WebQuestrubric.html.

 Filimentality Web-based Activity Tool. http://www.kn.att.com/wired/fil/.

Idea Generator. http://tommarch.com/learning/idea_machine.php.

Spartanburg: WebQuest Evaluation Form. http://www.spa3.k12.sc.us/ WebQuestrubric.htm.

Student Process Guides. http://projects.edtech.sandi.net/staffdev/tpss99/ processguides/index.htm.

WebQuest Generator. http://www.bestteachersites.com/web_tools/web_ quest/.

WebQuest Page. http://WebQuest.org/index.php.

What Are WebQuests Really? By Tom Marsh. http://bestWebQuests.com/ what_WebQuests_are.asp.

CHAPTER 4: CREATING A WEB INQUIRY ACTIVITY

How to Develop Inquiry Oriented Projects. http://www.youthlearn.org/ learning/activities/howto.asp.

Inquiry Page. http://inquiry.uiuc.edu/.

Library of Congress: American Memory Project. http://memory.loc.gov.

Web Inquiry Project. http://webinquiry.org/.

CHAPTER 5: CREATING A TELECOLLABORATIVE ACTIVITY

A Virtual Architecture's Web Home. http://virtual-architecture.wm.edu/index .html.

Classroom Projects listserv. http://www.globalschoolnet.org/.

Connect Teleprojects. http://exchange.co-nect.net/Teleprojects/.

ePals. http://www.epals.com/.

Global Grocery Project. http://landmark-project.com/ggl/index.html.

GLOBE (Global Learning and Observations to Benefit the Environment). http://www.globe.gov/.

Harris, J. (2001, May). Teachers as Telecollaborative Project Designers: A Curriculum-Based Approach. *Contemporary Issues in Technology and Teacher Education* 1(3). http://www.citejournal.org/vol1/iss3/seminal/article1.htm.

iEarn. http://www.iearn.org/projects/index.html.

KidLink. http://www.kidlink.org/.

KidProject. http://www.kidlink.org/KIDPROJ/.

Mining the Internet column, The Computing Teacher, Judi Harris. http://lrs .ed.uiuc.edu/Mining/April95-TCT.html.

Telecollaborative Learning Projects. http://www.2learn.ca/Projects/project centre/projintro.html.

CHAPTER 6: ASSESSMENTS AND INQUIRY

Rubistar. http://rubistar.4teachers.org/.

Rubrics for Teachers. http://www.rubrics4teachers.com/.

Using Rubrics in Middle School. http://www.middleweb.com/rubricsHG.html.

Why Use Rubrics. http://www.teach-nology.com/tutorials/teaching/rubrics/.

CHAPTER 7: INQUIRY IN EDUCATION USING TECHNOLOGY

Framework for 21st Century Learning. http://www.21stcenturyskills.org.

International Society for Technology in Education (ISTE). http://www.iste .org.

National Educational Technology Standards (NETS). http://www.iste.org/AM/ Template.cfm?Section=NETS.

Technology Integration Matrix. http://fcit.usf.edu/matrix/index.html.

ABOUT THE AUTHOR

Teresa Coffman has worked on both a middle school and high school level as a classroom teacher, technology coordinator, and director of academic technology. After completing her doctorate, she began teaching at the University of Mary Washington in Fredericksburg, Virginia. Currently she is an associate professor of education and teaches preservice teachers as they work toward initial licensure and a master's degree in education.